JAKARTA

History of a Misunderstood City

HERALD VAN DER LINDE

JAKARTA

History of a Misunderstood City

 Marshall Cavendish
Editions

Reprinted 2020

Published by Marshall Cavendish Editions
An imprint of Marshall Cavendish International

A member of the
Times Publishing Group

Other Marshall Cavendish Offices:
Marshall Cavendish Corporation, 800 Westchester Ave, Suite N-641, Rye Brook, NY 10573, USA • Marshall Cavendish International (Thailand) Co Ltd, 253 Asoke, 16th Floor, Sukhumvit 21 Road, Klongtoey Nua, Wattana, Bangkok 10110, Thailand • Marshall Cavendish (Malaysia) Sdn Bhd, Times Subang, Lot 46, Subang Hi-Tech Industrial Park, Batu Tiga, 40000 Shah Alam, Selangor Darul Ehsan, Malaysia

National Library Board, Singapore Cataloguing-in-Publication Data

Name(s): Van der Linde, Herald.
Title: Jakarta : history of a misunderstood city / Herald van der Linde.
Description: Singapore : Marshall Cavendish Editions, [2020] | Includes
    bibliographic references and index.
Identifier(s): OCN 1160890555 | ISBN 978-981-48-9348-0 (paperback)
Subject(s): LCSH: Jakarta (Indonesia)--History. | Jakarta (Indonesia)--Description
    and travel. | Jakarta (Indonesia)--Social conditions--History.
Classification: DDC 959.822--dc23

Front cover artwork by Derek Bacon (derekbacon.com)

Title page artwork by Rob Tuytel

Frontispiece: An engraving made in 1682 of the Tijgersgracht in Batavia by Johan Nieuhof.
Source: Atlas Van der Hagen, Koninklijke Bibliotheek, The Hague

Credits and permissions for the illustrations in this book are listed on pages xvii – xix

All maps by Brendan Whyte

Printed in Singapore

To my mom and dad,
my loving wife, Teni,
and my son, David

Contents

Map of the Region

to China,
Formosa
& Japan

to India
& Portugal

Malacca

S u m a t r a

B o r n e o,
K a l i m a n t a n

Pasei,
birthtown
of Fatahillah

to Amsterdam

Banten

Makas

Kelapa
Jayakarta
Batavia (1619-1943)
Jakarta

Jepara
Demak

Bali

Pakuan,
the town of Bujangga Manik

Kota Gede,
capital of the
Mataram Empire

| 0 | | | 1000 km |

| 0 | | | 600 miles |

The Indonesian archipelago, showing Jakarta (labelled with its earlier names) and
Malacca situated on key shipping lines. The Spice Islands are to the east.

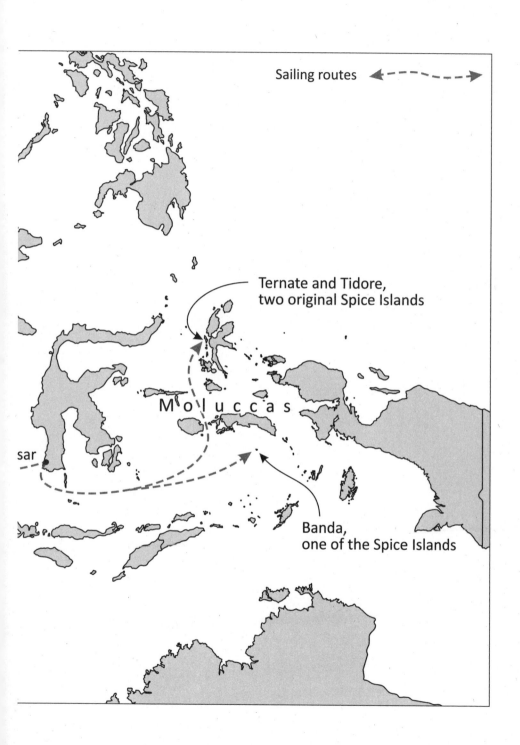

Sailing routes

Ternate and Tidore,
two original Spice Islands

Moluccas

Banda,
one of the Spice Islands

sar

Preface

If you have picked up this book, you must have at least a passing interest in Jakarta. Indonesia's capital is a fabulous place. To many, this statement might sound odd. The city conjures up images of endless traffic jams, hot, dusty roads, immense shopping malls that all sell pretty much the same thing, and, of course, floods.

But to me – an itinerant Dutchman – Jakarta is more than the political, economic, and cultural heart of Indonesia. This metropolis of more than 30 million people is a vibrant, bustling place, an immense labyrinth of small alleys and streets where children still walk to school, vendors sell *bakso* (meatball soup) and women operate tiny street-side stores stuffed with everything from snacks and noodles to batteries, cigarettes and stationery. There are small barber shops, motor repair shops – most advertising the ability to perform magic on any vehicle regardless of condition – badminton courts, and small mosques. Street traders effortlessly move vast quantities of goods around on motorcycles and handcarts through these intricate villages, or *kampung*.

At dusk, these small shops light up, creating an atmosphere of convivial good cheer. In the warm evenings, I enjoy sitting outside, smoking a *kretek* cigarette (a habit I am still trying to break) and order *sateh* or *nasi goreng* from the passing hawkers. This neighbourhood spirit harks back to the days when these *kampung* – now absorbed into the broader metropolis – were originally small villages and settlements set apart from the city.

JAKARTA

Jakartans are as diverse as they are friendly. It is difficult to find anyone who is not open for a chat, even with complete strangers. They come from all corners of the sprawling, multilingual Indonesian archipelago, bringing with them their own folklore, languages and dialects, traditions and cuisines. Every Jakartan knows where to get their noodles from Aceh, beef *rendang* from Padang or *coto*, a soup from Makassar in Sulawesi. Jakarta can leave its mark on visitors in many ways – whether by its sheer size, outrageous traffic congestion, imposing landmarks, or variety of colonial architecture – but its real beauty lies in the *kampung*.

The aim of this book is to make the city more accessible and enjoyable for tourists, occasional visitors, expats in the business community, and even long-term residents. Understanding its history is a great way to start. This is neither a historical treatise nor an academic study. It is a narrative woven with my own experiences, deep dives into the city's archives, the discovery of long-lost relatives, stories found in dusty old books written in Old Dutch, and the memories of family members, friends and acquaintances. Think of it as a patchwork quilt that stitches together personal observations, past events both momentous and long forgotten, a colourful cast of characters, and some very ancient history.

Much of this book is set against the broad sweep of the battle for colonial posessions in Asia that started in earnest around 1600. It traces the historical ups and downs of Jakarta, spanning the seventeeth to the twenty-first centuries. For the first half of this period the Dutch East India Company (the VOC) was all-powerful; later the city's fortunes were buffeted by the rise and fall of Napoleon Bonaparte. Later still, the green shoots of nationalism were nurtured by two violent world wars that eventually lead to the end of Dutch rule. In between, there are guest appearances by Captain James Cook, the great British explorer, and Sir Stamford Raffles, who went on to found Singapore. There are also juicy sex scandals, gory executions, a brutal massacre, an outbreak of deadly fever, bungled uprisings, murder most foul, and a particularly sadistic public flogging of the unfortunate daughter of a Dutch official. Much later on, a disastrous concert by English rock band Deep Purple gives a whole new meaning to the word head-banger.

This book is peopled by businessmen and women, complete and utter rogues, mistreated slaves, and ordinary citizens, rich and poor. Take for example Jan Pondard, a watchmaker who lived in the city in the early 1800s. The little we know about this man comes from two newspaper advertisements, one promoting his business and the other informing customers of his shop's move to another part of Batavia, the name the Dutch gave to what is now Jakarta. It is likely that he witnessed the British invasion of the city in 1811, so we can imagine his fear as soldiers marched right past his shop as they captured the city from the Dutch. Even with such meagre sources of information, we can paint a picture of what it must have been like, for a humble watchmaker, to live in the city at that time.

Another compelling personality is a young woman called Trijntje who arrived in 1622 from the Netherlands with a fine business head on her shoulders, and Si Pitung, a kind of local Robin Hood figure who lived in the city in the late 1800s. Others who make an appearance are still with us and offer dramatic eyewitness accounts of more recent events in the city from the last few decades.

And then there are the members of my own family. A few years ago, during a visit to Jakarta's archives, I stumbled across references to people with the same surname as me. One I know for certain is my great grandfather many times over — we are separated by about ten generations. Others are very likely to be family members. They were a very mixed bag: some were successful, another ended up in a miserable marriage, and one girl died in poverty in Batavia's orphanage. Still more witnessed and may have even taken part in one of the city's darkest events, the massacre of the Chinese population in 1740. It was digging into these archives that provided me with the inspiration for this book.

But enough of the past. What does the future hold for this great city? Jakarta faces immense challenges. It floods regularly at enormous cost to residents and parts of the city are slowly subsiding into the mud. There is also a big wealth gap and the poor are far too often pushed to the fringes of society. This book does not pretend to offer big picture solutions — we'll leave that to the politicians, urban planners, architects, engineers and economists.

Yet the ingenuity of the people who live here is remarkable. History tells us that the city has bounced back from adversity on numerous occasions. Residents have come back together after massacres and riots, rebuilt neighbourhoods after floods and re-invented parts of the city which had become uninhabitable. The people of Jakarta have an extraordinary ability to rebound from even the grimmest of circumstances.

This book makes mention of places that don't exist anymore but also plenty of others that do and that are well worth a visit. They include Kota, the old town of Batavia, and the Portuguese church outside the old city walls in an area now called Gereja Sion. A few old colonial estates along the old Molenvliet road (now Jl. Hayam Wuruk/Jl. Gajah Madah) as well as the atmospheric Pancoran Tea House are still around.

After visiting the famous landmarks, be sure to wander around the places that capture the essence and the soul of this city — Jakarta's labyrinthine and magical *kampung*.

Herald van der Linde

June 2020

Hong Kong

A Note on Non-English Terms

The aim of this book is to make Jakarta a more accessible and enjoyable city to visitors and residents alike. With that in mind, decisions with regard to names, references and spelling were made to make reading easier.

The term "Jakarta" refers to an administrative unit with precise boundaries. Depok is just south of Jakarta and Bogor is another city. Over time, these satellite towns became glued to the growing city and are now effectively part of the larger conurbation, "Jabodetabek", an acronym for Jakarta-Bogor-Depok-Tangerang-Bekasi. In the book, we loosely refer to this agglomeration as Jakarta.

In the text, Malay refers to the older version of Indonesian that was spoken across the archipelago. Indonesian as a language used today, Bahasa Indonesia, is actually a codified version of Malay.

In modern Indonesian, the word for street is *jalan*, often abbreviated to "Jl.". Thus, Theewater Straat (in Dutch) is in English Teawater Street and in Indonesian Jl. Teh. Current Indonesian spelling has been used for place names and streets. Thus, instead of the colonial Passer Baroe or Pasar Baroe, this book uses Pasar Baru, as this is how the place is known today. We also refer to Bogor although at the time, the Dutch name was Buitenzorg. Sometimes it is quite obvious that two words stand for the same place, such as Harmonie in Dutch referring to today's Harmoni, a well-known junction in Central Jakarta, just north of the presidential palace in south Petojo.

Knowledge of a few Indonesian words can help make reading street names a bit easier. *Besar* (large) and *kecil* (small) often show up in street names and in such cases might refer to the size of the road or mean either "main" or "secondary". A *pintu* is a door or a gate. There are also regular references to *kampung*, which is a mostly rural settlement, somewhere in between a hamlet and a town. A town or city is a *kota*. Other names commonly found on maps are *sawah*, a paddy field, and *rawa*, which means a marsh or swamp. These names adorn many signposts across the city and remind us of the bogs and fields that used to litter the area.

There are also Dutch names in this book. Some might be difficult to pronounce. Trijntje, for example, is pronounced as "trin-tee" and the name Coen is pronounced as "koon". The "ch" in the name Chastelein is pronounced like the "ch" in Bach. The letter "d" or "z" at the end of a name indicates the position of son or daughter. Thus Trijntje Willemsd is "Trijntje, the daughter of Willem".

List of Illustrations

Engraving of the Tijgersgracht in Batavia by Johan Nieuhoff. *Koninklijke Bibliotheek, The Hague*

Artist's impression of ships at port of Batavia. © *Rob Tuytel*

Map of the island of Java, 1596. Anonymous, 1646. *Rijksmuseum Amsterdam*

View of Batavia, painting by Hendrick Jacobsz. Doubles, 1640–1676. *Rijksmuseum Amsterdam*

Etching and engraving of the city, attributed to printmaker Adriaen Matham, 1646. *Rijksmuseum Amsterdam*

Artist's impression of the market square with early version of town hall, circa 1628. © *Rob Tuytel*

Map of Batavia dated 1627. *Westfries Museum, Hoorn, the Netherlands*

The Castle of Batavia, painting by Andries Beeckman, circa 1661. *Rijksmuseum Amsterdam*

Medal presented to Jacques Specx, 1632. *Rijksmuseum Amsterdam*

Etching and engraving of Fort Noordwijk in Jakarta, Jacob van der Schley, 1747–1779. *Rijksmuseum Amsterdam*

Drawing of Fort de Waterplaats at the Molenvliet, possibly by A. de Nelly, 1762–1783. *Rijksmuseum Amsterdam*

Photograph of the Pieter Erberveld monument in Batavia, circa 1910. *KITLV, Leiden University Libraries Digital Collections*

Etching of the 1740 Chinese massacre, Jacob van der Schley, after Adolf van der Laan, 1761–1763. *Rijksmuseum Amsterdam*

JAKARTA

Theevisite in een Europees huis in Batavia, drawing by Jan Brandes, 1779–1785. *Rijksmuseum Amsterdam*

Huis en landgoed Brandes buiten Batavia, drawing by Jan Brandes, 1785. *Rijksmuseum Amsterdam*

Drawing of Batavia circa 1770–1772, presumably by Johannes Rach. *KITLV, Leiden University Libraries Digital Collections*

Picture postcard featuring the Reinier de Klerk house, circa 1930. *KITLV, Leiden University Libraries Digital Collections*

Image of Weltevreden Waterlooplein, published by G. Kolff & Co between 1906 and 1930. *KITLV, Leiden University Libraries Digital Collections*

Advertisement placed by J. Pondard. *Java Government Gazette*

Photograph of *ondel-ondel* puppets, Gunawan Kartapranata, 2011. *creativecommons.org/licenses/by-sa/3.0/legalcode*

Image of Harmonie Club and Oger, published by Boekhandel Visser & Co. between 1895 and 1908. *KITLV, Leiden University Libraries Digital Collections*

Picture postcard featuring Hotel des Indes, published circa 1936. *KITLV, Leiden University Libraries Digital Collections*

Image of Raden Saleh house, published by Woodbury & Page circa 1867. *KITLV, Leiden University Libraries Digital Collections*

Image of private colonial house, published by Woodbury & Page circa 1870. *KITLV, Leiden University Libraries Digital Collections*

Image of two men on veranda with servants, published circa 1917. *KITLV, Leiden University Libraries Digital Collections*

Photograph of a *nyai* with child, anonymous, circa 1870–circa 1880. *Rijksmuseum Amsterdam*

Picture postcard featuring tram in Gondangdia, published circa 1910. *KITLV, Leiden University Libraries Digital Collections*

Picture postcard featuring Pasar Baru, published circa 1936. *KITLV, Leiden University Libraries Digital Collections*

List of Illustrations

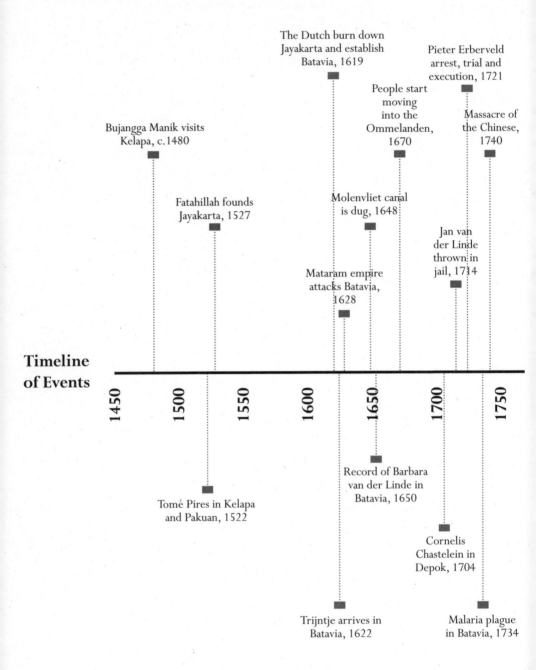

The Dutch burn down
Jayakarta and establish
Batavia, 1619

Pieter Erberveld
arrest, trial and
execution, 1721

People start
moving
into the
Ommelanden,
1670

Massacre of
the Chinese,
1740

Bujangga Manik visits
Kelapa, c.1480

Fatahillah founds
Jayakarta, 1527

Molenvliet canal
is dug, 1648

Jan van
der Linde
thrown in
jail, 1714

Mataram empire
attacks Batavia,
1628

**Timeline
of Events**

1450   1500   1550   1600   1650   1700   1750

Record of Barbara
van der Linde in
Batavia, 1650

Tomé Pires in Kelapa
and Pakuan, 1522

Cornelis
Chastelein in
Depok, 1704

Trijntje arrives in
Batavia, 1622

Malaria plague
in Batavia, 1734

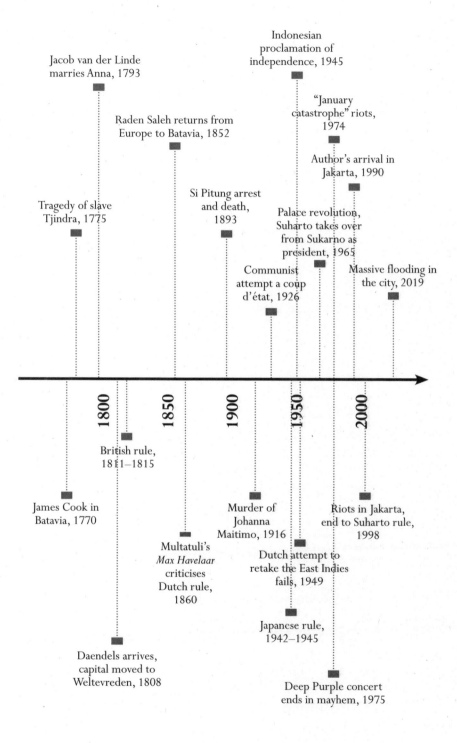

Jacob van der Linde marries Anna, 1793

Indonesian proclamation of independence, 1945

Raden Saleh returns from Europe to Batavia, 1852

"January catastrophe" riots, 1974

Author's arrival in Jakarta, 1990

Tragedy of slave Tjindra, 1775

Si Pitung arrest and death, 1893

Palace revolution, Suharto takes over from Sukarno as president, 1965

Communist attempt a coup d'état, 1926

Massive flooding in the city, 2019

1800

1850

1900

1950

2000

British rule, 1811–1815

James Cook in Batavia, 1770

Murder of Johanna Maitimo, 1916

Riots in Jakarta, end to Suharto rule, 1998

Multatuli's *Max Havelaar* criticises Dutch rule, 1860

Dutch attempt to retake the East Indies fails, 1949

Japanese rule, 1942–1945

Daendels arrives, capital moved to Weltevreden, 1808

Deep Purple concert ends in mayhem, 1975

Map of Present-Day Greater Jakarta

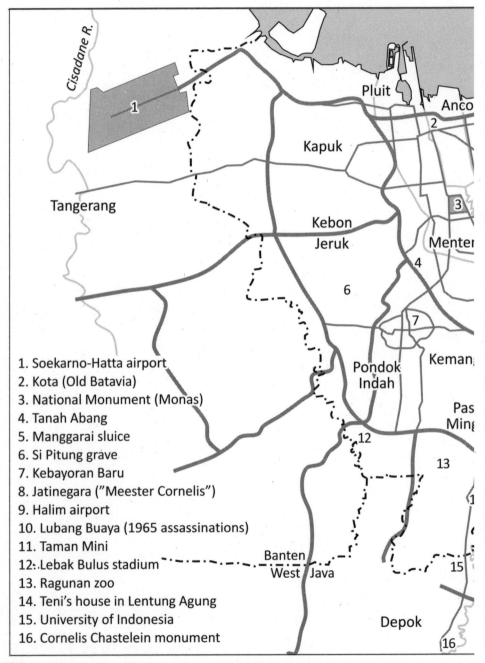

1. Soekarno-Hatta airport
2. Kota (Old Batavia)
3. National Monument (Monas)
4. Tanah Abang
5. Manggarai sluice
6. Si Pitung grave
7. Kebayoran Baru
8. Jatinegara ("Meester Cornelis")
9. Halim airport
10. Lubang Buaya (1965 assassinations)
11. Taman Mini
12. Lebak Bulus stadium
13. Ragunan zoo
14. Teni's house in Lentung Agung
15. University of Indonesia
16. Cornelis Chastelein monument

The present-day greater Jakarta area, showing landmarks and major ring roads.
Near the centre the Manggarai sluice directs river water around the city.

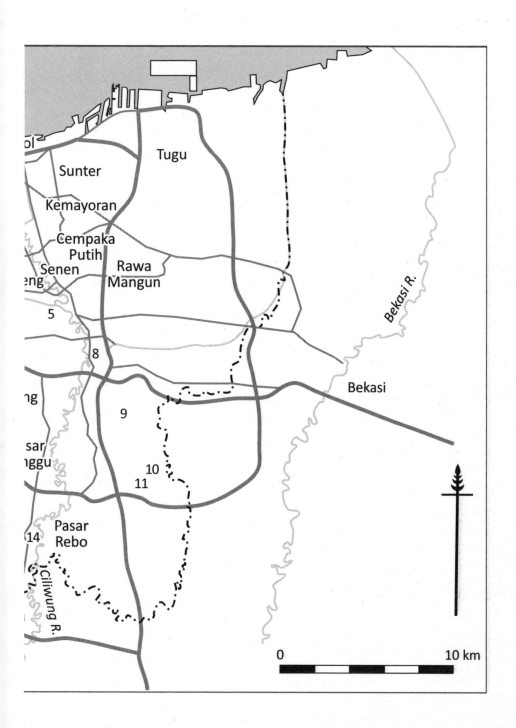

Tugu

Sunter

Kemayoran

Cempaka
Putih

Senen

Rawa
Mangun

eng

5

8

9

10

11

Pasar
Rebo

14

J.Ciliwung R.

ng

sar
nggu

Bekasi

Bekasi R.

0   10 km

A Word of Warning, a Fortuitous Meeting and a New Home
1990–2000

"Avoid it, at least as a first point of entry."

That was the first advice I was given about Jakarta. As a 19-year-old student I had saved some money and decided to spend it on a low-budget backpacking trip to Indonesia, my first trip outside Europe. It was 1990.

The advice came from my uncle who had visited the city several times. In all fairness, he was not suggesting that I avoid Jakarta entirely, but that I should start my trip in peaceful Bali rather than plunge into the sound and fury of Jakarta. He thought I should save the capital for the end of the trip.

And so I did. I bought my tickets and in August flew to Bali via Singapore. I vividly remember my very first impression of Indonesia. Upon descending the airplane stairs, I stood still on the tarmac and inhaled an incredible concoction of aromas – a mixture of ripe fruit, fried meat, wet grass and burned rubber.

I hopped around Bali for a few weeks and made my way east across a string of islands. On a ferry trip between Bali and the neighbouring island of Lombok I came across a family visiting friends. Their 9-year-old daughter was seasick, and I gave her an aspirin. A few hours later, we landed at the southern tip of Lombok. I had planned to take a bus north-east to visit a few quiet beaches and start my exploration of the island from there. On my way to the bus terminal, a passing car honked, slowed and the tinted windows were lowered. It was the family of the little girl and they asked me if I wanted to come with them to Mataram, the capital of Lombok. As it was on my way to the beaches, I jumped in.

A problem immediately started to manifest itself – I did not speak Indonesian. Before I left I had followed a television course in the language, but all I remembered were a few words. I was far from conversational. In the end that did not matter. My willingness to struggle with the language combined with the friendliness and patience on the side of the Indonesian family and their friends ensured that we got on very well. In the end, I decided to stay a few days in Mataram and the family took me to local restaurants, taught me more Indonesian, introduced me to a variety of local dishes and showed me around town.

When we parted they made me promise to visit them in Jakarta, where they lived. I then continued my journey to some of the other islands in east Indonesia. A few months later I hobbled into Jakarta by train, arriving at Gambir, the train station right in the city centre. My first views of the city were the houses and gardens that lined the rail tracks, the clothes hanging in the sun to dry, children running along with the train and the large line of cars piled up at the level crossing, waiting for the train to pass.

After I checked into a backpacker hostel, I called my Indonesian friends and a few hours later I found myself in a house in Pasar Minggu, a district in south Jakarta, surrounded by the whole family and their friends. A few neighbours popped in to say hello to this somewhat dishevelled Dutch fellow. In the months and years thereafter I would repeatedly stay in their home, become close friends with the rest of the family and improve my language skills. Meanwhile, I started to explore the rest of the city. I took buses around town and got to know the various districts where some of my new Indonesian friends lived – Tanah Abang, Menteng, Kalibata, Blok M, Slipi, Depok and Jatinegara.

A Word of Warning, a Fortuitous Meeting and a New Home

I'd learned about the Dutch East Indies at school but was surprised to find so many remnants of the colonial past. There were old Dutch buildings, some Dutch words were still in use in Bahasa Indonesia and, despite a colonial period that stretched over nearly 350 years, a generally positive disposition towards Belanda, the term used to refer to the Dutch. Also, many people I met had family in the Netherlands.

Repeated return visits over the following years allowed me to soak up Indonesian culture, become fluent in Bahasa Indonesia and gradually discover an affection for Jakarta, that urban jungle I had avoided as a port of entry on my very first trip. But that first time will always have a special place in my heart.

****

After a gap of a few years, following my graduation from a Dutch university with a degree in economics, I decided to try my luck in Jakarta in 1995. I found myself working for a bank in the city and living with a few other foreigners that I had befriended. During the weekends, I would visit my first Indonesian friends in south Jakarta.

I used my holidays to explore lesser known parts of the archipelago, from Nias, an island off the coast of Sumatra in the west of the country, to Flores in east Indonesia. In 1997, on a plane back to Jakarta I found myself chatting with one of the other passengers, a rather attractive Indonesian lady of my age. Later, at the luggage conveyor belt, I saw her again and was brave enough to ask for her name – Teni – and her mobile phone number.

For months I tried to meet up with her, but every time I tried, Teni told me she was travelling. Eventually I decided that she was probably avoiding me. In a last attempt, I decided to do something that is rather uncommon today – I sent her a postcard with a few friendly comments and my telephone number. The ball was in her court.

It worked. Teni called back. Two weeks later, we met at the O-la-la Café in south Jakarta's Blok M. A few months later, we were backpacking together across Ternate, Tidore and Banda, the famed Spice Islands in the Moluccas in east Indonesia.

One day, she asked me to come to her home in south Jakarta. And so, on a Sunday morning in October 1997, I made my way to meet the family for the very first time. Upon arrival at her home in Lenteng Agung, I found her father sitting outside his home drawing slowly on a thick, white Dji Sam Soe *kretek* cigarette. He had one daughter and four sons and was quite eager to meet the man who had caught his only daughter's eye.

When I approached, he stood up, introduced himself and asked, "You are Dutch, aren't you?" in Indonesian. Upon confirmation, he told me that he had shot at the Dutch in Indonesia's war of independence. I responded by saying that I hoped he would not make a habit of it.

Over the following months I would meet uncles, aunts, nephews, nieces and all kinds of other, less easily identifiable extended family members. Some of the older generation greeted me in fluent Dutch, spoken with a beautiful Indonesian-styled staccato and a rich vocabulary common in 1930s Dutch schools. Some had fought in the war against the Dutch in the late 1940s. But with the incredible hospitality typical of Indonesians, they considered this more of a reason to bond than to stress our differences. "We have been friends for over 350 years," they joked. I was made very welcome in the family. Teni and I married in 2000.

****

My own grandfather had told me that our family had a history in Indonesia, but nobody was sure who they were and where they had lived. I decided to visit the national archive to see if I could find some fossilised evidence of these ancestors. For some people, going through archives sounds like an act of self-flagellation, but I loved it. With a great sense of excitement I poured over masses of old documents, looking at the stories that they held: divorces, wills, church records and files of court cases, all written down centuries ago.

For two days I flipped through old files and catalogues of the city archives of Batavia (what Jakarta used to be called by the Dutch colonial masters), when I came across the following commentary:

> Johannes van der Linde, senior merchant and captain of administration at the castle, born in Batavia on 5 Feb 1707 and died 15 Oct 1742. His family coat of arms is in the Church in Zwolle.[1]

This, I knew, was an ancestor as he was mentioned in a family book that I had read in the Netherlands.[2] And our family coat of arms is still in a church in Zwolle, a city in the eastern part of the country. I had discovered a direct connection, an arch between the two of us spanning about ten generations.

Thrilled, I went looking for more evidence and in the next few days I found a few more entries labelled "van der Linde" in the Batavia city archives. The earliest record I found was of a Barbara van der Linde who, together with her husband, arrived by ship in Batavia in 1650. In 1710, another Van der Linde was recorded as a carpenter and in 1714 another, possibly his brother, was thrown in jail after failing to pay his debts. Either one might have been the father of the senior merchant who was born in 1707. In 1798, there was an entry for Jacob van der Linde as the chief surgeon at a city hospital, which still exists today. In 1861, one Van der Linde started a business with a man called Leendert Bras. In 1916, another started a trading company with someone named Teves; the Linde-Teves enterprise seemed to have flourished.

How would the city have looked in their day? Would I be able to recognise some of the houses or buildings where they had lived and worked? If they wanted to go for a cold beer or dinner, where would they have gone?

Thus, I set out to get to know the history of Jakarta, the city I had got to know so well, where I had made so many good friends, met my wife and where my ancestors had made a living over the last few centuries. The idea was to dive into archives and university libraries to find more books, stories and evidence that, put together, would create a story of this city as made by the people who lived in it.

This book is the result of my endeavours. It's not a conventional history book, but rather, an attempt to introduce this much-maligned city to a broader audience who may, like me, learn to love Jakarta.

Whenever Jakarta comes up in conversations, most people tell me what they don't like about the city. It's crowded and lacking in parks and open spaces; most entertainment is found in the city's large shopping malls; traffic is a nightmare. I have to admit they have a point. But there is so much more to the city than congested roads and endless malls. What makes Jakarta so enjoyable are its people and the many stories that have unfolded over the centuries. The city's quieter allure lies in the small alleys and roads that run through the *kampung*, spinning a large cobweb which surrounds the skeleton of Jakarta – its thoroughfares, highways, ring roads, museums and monuments. Call it the Jakarta's soul or consciousness, it is here, in the *kampung*, that the real beauty of this city is found: vivid, ethereal, and hidden in plain sight.

I hope this book will allow readers to gain a better appreciation of the city. I hope it will inspire a reader to get a taste of its rich history by visiting the National Museum to learn about Hindu and Buddhist culture and the lifestyle of the early humans who inhabited the area. Or delve into the colonial era by checking out the old buildings dating back to the days of the Vereenigde Oostindische Compagnie (VOC) – the Dutch East India Company – the trading giant that dominated the spice trade and saw off the British in that part of the world. Some are now home to the Museum Bahari, the maritime museum in the old Sunda Kelapa harbour area.

Alternatively, visit the Museum Taman Prasasti, a cemetery built by the Dutch colonial government in 1795 as a resting place for their prominent countrymen. Among the impressive array of tombstones, there is a skull embedded in one of the walls, a story related to a Batavian conspiracy in the early 1700s. Then there is the Reinier de Klerk mansion, the home of a former Governor-General of the East Indies. It was later owned by an illiterate Pole who had to hide his Jewish identity and lived a remarkable rags-to-riches story. Beaten as a servant in the mansion, he swore he would eventually own the property, which he did after a successful career with the VOC.

This book traces the evolution of Jakarta from pre-colonial times to the giant metropolis it is today. In each chapter, we look at some of the people who walked its streets and, insofar as history and archives allow us, try to follow their lives.

Chapter 1 starts with the oldest available evidence of people living in the area we now call Jakarta: script chiselled onto a stone around the fifth century. It takes a look at life in the city of Kelapa, which was renamed Jayakarta in 1527. After repeated wars for influence over this city, the Dutch took control in 1619, establishing their own city of Batavia. Chapter 2 features an entrepreneurial lady named Trijntje, who arrived in Batavia in 1622 and survived an unsuccessful attempt by a Javanese army to wipe Batavia from the map.

Chapter 3 shows the city spreading into the regions surrounding Batavia in the later 1600s; in Chapter 4, we see the negative consequences of this sprawl as the city faced a mysterious disease in the 1730s and witnessed an orgy of violence in 1740. In Chapter 5 we meet Captain Cook, who was not impressed by the city in 1770, and discover how Weltevreden, located a little further south, became Batavia's playground for the rich.

In Chapter 6, watchmaker Jan Pondard witnesses the arrival of the British in 1811 and their retreat a few years later. Chapter 7 features the legendary Si Pitung, Jakarta's own Robin Hood, and the rise of Indonesian nationalism in the 1880s. Chapter 8 compares the city to a kettle on slow boil, with racial and class tensions highlighted by the murder of Johanna Maitimo in 1916.

Chapter 9 is about crowd control. After Indonesian independence in 1945, Jakarta experienced an explosive population growth as people from all over the archipelago poured in. The last chapter ponders the city's challenges and how it might rise to meet them in the future.

But let's go to the beginning.

It all started with the discovery of a stone.

Chapter 1
From Kelapa to Batavia
Pre-1619

Compared to some of the largest islands in Indonesia, Java is small. The spine of this slender strip of land comprises a string of volcanoes that nourishes its soil, moistens its rivers and has a penchant for sudden eruptions. Add to this the throbbing heat and intensity of the tropical sun and the result is one of the most fertile places on our planet. On its western edge, the Salak and Gede mountains are also the birthplaces of five large rivers – the Cisadane, the Angke, the Ciliwung, the Bekasi and the Citarum – that spread out like a fan from current-day Bogor towards the northern seashores. *Ci* means "river" in Sundanese, so Citarum is the river Tarum.

This fecund land has been inhabited since Neolithic times but it is difficult to exactly pinpoint when and where the first humans settled down in the area that we now define as Jakarta or "Jabodetabek", an acronym that sews together Jakarta with the surrounding cities of Bogor, Depok, Tangerang, and Bekasi. But while the time frames and locations of these first human settlements in what we call Greater Jakarta are clouded by history, there are some artefacts left from those days.

One day in 1863, not far from the city of Bogor, close to Ciampea in what is currently Kampung Muara, a Javanese man walked along a river and spotted a huge bolder with inscriptions of two large feet and sinuous, curvy writing on its smooth surface. Scholars were called in to take a closer

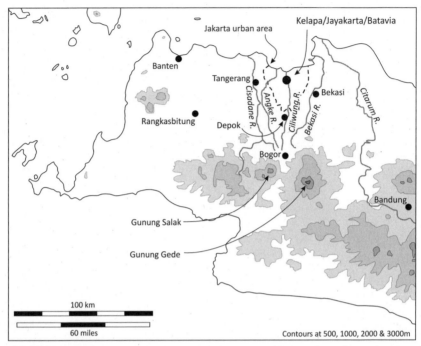

Map of the western part of Java, showing the five rivers – the Cisadane, the Angke, the Ciliwung, the Bekasi and the Citarum – flowing from the mountains, Gunung Salak and Gunung Gede.

look at these strange, alien-looking messages and eventually identified it as Pallava, a script in use thousands of miles away across the Indian Ocean in southern India. The inscription was translated as follows:

> The powerful, illustrious and brave King the famous Purnawarman
> (of the) Tarumanagara (kingdom) whose (print of the) foot soles
> are the same (as those of) God Wishnu.[1]

How a large boulder came to be inscribed in a language from across an ocean, thousands of miles away, can be traced to travel and commerce. In the fifth century, sailor-traders along the coast of Sumatra, Java, and Kalimantan made acquaintance with merchant communities in Indian ports, exchanging anything from fruits to cloth, cotton, axes, turtle shells, feathers and spices. Around the same time, Indian traders who sailed around the Indonesian archipelago found it worthwhile to establish local branches in their trading network where they left people behind to secure regular supplies of regional specialties to their markets. They paid tribute to the local heads of these ports who in return adopted Indian royal titles such as raja or maharaja, or adding the royal suffix -varman, to their names, as these were familiar to Indian merchants with whom they traded. Just like King Purnawarman.[2]

These Indian traders brought with them Hindu and Buddhist ideas and the Sanskrit and Pallava scripts. Some of it seeped into the Sundanese and Javanese languages, which explains the writing on that large boulder. The boulder came to be known as the Ciaruteun inscription and it still lies where the Javanese farmer had discovered it well over a century ago.

King Purnawarman appears to have been a prolific builder and was eager to leave evidence of his power and achievements for posterity. It seems he ordered more of these stones to be chiselled with statements and so far seven have been discovered. These chiselled pillars were large and immovable, and archaeologists have postulated that they might have been focal points for ceremonies in open spaces. The oldest of these stones, the Prasasti Tugu, was discovered in the small town of Tugu and is currently on display in the National Museum in Jakarta. The writing on it tells us about the slaughter of a thousand cows to celebrate the opening of a long canal. It also mentions that at that time Purnawarman had already been on the throne for about 22 years.[3]

Assuming that it did not make sense to dig a canal in the middle of nowhere and that waterworks of this type required a huge amount of manpower, it is reasonable to say that there must have been a flourishing city worthy of a stone inscription for future generations to read about it. These large boulders then, are the very first artefacts pointing to the existance of a city in the area that we now call Greater Jakarta.

We now know that this city was called Sunda Pura ("Sunda city"), and was probably located near present-day Bekasi in east Jakarta. Even now, the people in West Java are referred to as Sundanese. The people in Sunda Pura grew bananas, cucumbers, onions, ginger, and garlic and raised fish, ducks, and chickens. They also enjoyed alcoholic drinks made from palm and sugarcane and at ceremonies, they feasted on rice, chicken, and vegetables on palm leaves. This city was a focal point in a commercial network of villages and ports across West Java from which professional vendors operated. They were buyers of cows, goats, buffaloes and pigs and sold these in nearby villages. Farmers would trade rice, fruit, cotton, clothing, salted fish, and cooking oils in local village markets. In particularly strong demand were locally made stone axes, a handy tool for farmers living in and close to rainforests, who needed them to fell trees and clear undergrowth. Archaeologists have discovered[4] that axes were made even well before the era of Tarumanegara and Sunda Pura, at ancient sites in what is now south Jakarta: Pejaten, Condet, Tanjung Barat and Kelapa Dua.

****

Kingdoms came and went, and by around 1300, it was the Pajajaran empire that ruled over large parts of West Java. It was in the days of this kingdom that Indonesians would notice new groups of traders on the international trading circuit. These were Muslim traders from Arabia, India, and China who arrived with increasing frequency at ports dotted along the archipelago. They brought with them the Islamic religion, carried with them books written in the Arabic alphabet, and valued the title of sultan over raja. At the same time, Indonesian merchants went and sold goods in Indian ports controlled by Muslim merchants, increasing the number of touchpoints these Indonesians had with Islam. The religion became increasingly popular, culminating in 1470, when Demak in Central Java was proclaimed a Muslim kingdom.[5]

It was in the twelfth century, just before the rise of the Pajajaran empire, that there was the first report of a harbour town called Sunda Kelapa,[6] a name that referred not only to the Sundanese empire but also to the *kelapa*, or coconut, presumably because of the abundance of these lanky trees along the seashore. Today, Sunda Kelapa is still a small district in the very north of Jakarta. The very first foreign mention of Kelapa is on a fourteenth-century Chinese map, where it is called "Chia Liu Pa". At the time, Kelapa was a small entrepot for traders and sailors who stocked up on rice, cloth, and pepper in the seaside town and then sailed around the archipelago. These traders were dependent on the monsoons; they would sail in one particular direction during one monsoon and conduct business, buy new goods, repair their ships and wait until the monsoon winds changed, allowing them to navigate their vessels back home.

But while Kelapa was an important trading hub, it was not where the Sundanese royals of the Pajajaran empire lived.[7] They preferred to withdraw to a fortified court in the cool, leafy foothills of Mount Salak in what is now the Batu Tulis district in Bogor. From Kelapa, it was a two-day walk to Pakuan, the capital of the Pajajaran empire. And it is here, in the foothills of the mountain, where probably one of the first accounts of the city of Kelapa is found, written down by a lonely travelling prince-monk who grew up in Pakuan. We know of this monk because of the existence of his writings on old palm leaves, presented to the Bodleian library in Oxford, England in 1627 by a merchant called Andrew James.[8] A Dutch scholar of Sundanese languages, Dr J. Noorduyn, rediscovered these palm leaves in 1968 and started translating them, bringing back to life the story of the wandering prince-monk from Pakuan. His name was Bujangga Manik.

In the latter part of the fifteenth century, this young Sundanese prince decided that the royal life of lavish feasting on the cool slopes of Mount Salak was just not for him. He preferred to live the life of a man of religion and decided to leave Pakuan to wander alone around Java. He made two journeys, both on foot and each covering well over a thousand kilometres.

It is through his writings that we get a first-hand glimpse of Java in the fifteenth century. He detailed the mountains he saw, the rivers he crossed and the villages he frequented. He travelled all over Java and then crossed the sea to Bali, which he judged to be a dreadfully busy place (despite being centuries before the days of mass tourism and regular visits by Australian rugby league clubs in search of rest and recreation). Somewhere on his travels he met a female ascetic, who asked if he could be an elder brother and mentor to her. At a minimum, that would suggest that they travel together. But Bujangga Manik was not tempted. He held up a book and said, "Just like fire when it comes near to palm fibre, it will surely inflame, thus it is with men and women."[9] With that, he continued his journey alone.

He then made his way back from east Java by boat and after half a month's sailing, reached the port of Kelapa. Although he does not mention it, small local boats, *perahu*, would have littered the bay, full of goods to sell in the market. He would also have seen large Chinese junks, the pan-regional bulk carriers of the day.

Eventually, he stepped ashore at Kelapa, situated on the west bank at the mouth of the Ciliwung River. He might well have stayed there for a few days to soak up the atmosphere but the ascetic monk did not relish places with lots of people. Still, he would have seen the wooden houses covered with roofs made of palm leaves that stretched out along the riverfront into the interior. In the rainy season, the whole area turned into a large swamp. It was a crowded place and no surprise that fires regularly damaged parts of the city.

As he walked the streets and alleys that criss-crossed the town, he would have seen people selling rice, vegetables, fruits, pepper, cloth, and meats. Many of these people would have been local Sundanese, but there were also Chinese, Arabs, Tamils, Gujaratis, and Malays. These foreigners were mostly sailors waiting for monsoon winds to change in their favour. They were allowed to stay outside the walled city, gathering regularly at the equivalent of a local tavern, probably nothing more than a small wooden shack, where *arak* (rice wine) and other alcoholic beverages were for sale.

Walking further, Bujangga Manik would have seen that the streets opened up to a large square and an adjacent large wooden palace for the prince of Kelapa. This prince paid tribute to the King of Sunda who lived in the cool, lush mountains of Pakuan further south. But Bujangga Manik made surprisingly few references to all this. Instead, he wrote about how he made his way to Pakuan and crossed the Ciliwung River several times while visiting eleven towns, which suggests that the area surrounding Kelapa was already well populated.

All the villages and towns he mentioned are long gone, except one. A town he visited is referred to as Ancol Tamiang which, he writes, is located near a great forest. This is probably current-day Ancol in north Jakarta, these days better known for its large theme park.

Elsewhere he mentioned crossing the Cileungsi River, which still flows northward through Greater Jakarta towards Bekasi. He also came across the Citarum, the river that now traces the eastern perimeter of Greater Jakarta.

He eventually arrived in Pakuan and saw his mother, who was overjoyed at his return. Here, he was tempted again, this time by a young princess. Things got a little steamy: she offered him a betel nut which she prepared by rolling the leaves and nut over her thighs and breasts and by binding them with a thread from her dress, as "to bind a young man, to excite a bachelor's desire".[10] But the monk wouldn't have any of it, refusing to be lured back into the luxurious life of a prince. Bujangga Manik eventually settled on a mountain somewhere in West Java where he spent the rest of his life – alone.

This then is probably one of the earliest written records of the city of Kelapa, enscribed on palm leaves in the last part of the fifteenth century. More frequent mentions of the city Kelapa appeared when Portuguese traders arrived in the archipelago.

****

The Portuguese arrived in Southeast Asia in the early 1500s and initially focused their attention on Malacca, a key node in the Asian maritime trade network on Malaysia's western coast. New foreigners arriving in Malacca were nothing new – the Chinese, Gujaratis, Tamils, Javanese, and Sumatrans had all preceded the Portuguese. These foreign traders assimilated into Malaccan society, often marrying local women and gradually infusing the local culture with the culture and traditions they brought with them. Any dealings these foreigners had with the local king or sultan were conducted through the Kapitein of their communities.

But this coexistence was not always peaceful. In 1511, the Portuguese decided to take things in their own hands. They laid siege to Malacca for 40 days, after which they were able to enter and pillage the city and make it their own. After taking control, they kicked out the Muslim traders, who were the biggest trade rivals and now had to look elsewhere for an alternative base. Kelapa seemed a good alternative where the Muslim traders could conduct their business without interference from the Portuguese. This was not to last: a few years later the Portuguese set their eyes on Kelapa too, in search of its fabled peppers.

When the first Portuguese ships anchored off the coast of Kelapa,

From Kelapa to Batavia

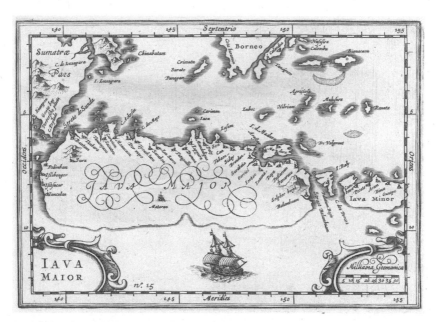

Map of the island of Java, circa 1596. Titled "Iava Maior", a distinction is made between Java Major and Java Minor (this is the island of Sumbawa). Jakarta (spelled as "Iacatra") is located on the northwestern coast of Java Major.

Detail of the map above, showing Jakarta spelled as "Iacatra".

they stepped right into a geopolitical hornet's nest. At the time, two new competing kingdoms were on the rise: Banten to the west of Kelapa and Demak to its east. With this threat in mind, it is understandable why the local ruler of Kelapa showed great interest in the firepower that the Portuguese carried with them and why he was open to Portuguese demands for a fort in town.

Thus, an agreement to ensure the defence of Kelapa was signed on 21 August 1522 by Portuguese representative Henrique Leme and the Sundanese king, commonly known as Ratu Sang Hyang. In return, the Portuguese got about a thousand sacks of pepper. In the Portuguese fashion of the day, to mark the event, they hammered a *padrão*, a large stone marker, into the ground. Over time, this stone was lost but in 1918, during the erection of a new building in north Jakarta, construction workers discovered the elongated stone with Portuguese inscriptions that read "The Lord of Portugal, The Hope of The World".[11] The stone is now on display at the National Museum in central Jakarta.

One of the Portuguese men wandering around Kelapa in 1522 was Tomé Pires, an apothecary from Lisbon with an eye for detail and a habit of noting down his impressions, which allowed him later to publish a real doorstopper with the title *Suma Oriental*. He explored the town of Kelapa and gives us a glimpse of what it must have looked like. He described the town as a magnificent port with courts, clerks and traders busy selling peppers, rice, vegetables, fruits, livestock, slaves, and cloth. Pires must have been impressed because he noted that "it was the largest and best port of all".

Tomé Pires also made an effort to see the famed Pakuan in the foothills of the nearby mountains, a journey that took him two days, just like Bujangga Manik a few decades earlier. In the *Suma Oriental*, he wrote of dense forests with trees that had branches reaching to the ground, pigs, buffalos, stags, and counts forty elephants. Upon arrival in Pakuan he observed that the houses were well built from wood and palm leaves. He also noted that the Sundanese were heathens but, despite this, they were "chivalrous, of good figure, swarthy and robust".[12] These Sundanese traded in long pepper (presumably chili), tamarind and slaves. Shops along the roads sold rice, vegetables, pigs, goats, cows, wines and fruits. For trading, cash was used, a kind of pierced coin, presumably imported from China. When he asked locals what the city's name was, people misunderstood him. Instead of "Pakuan", they told him this was the royal city, "Dayeuh" in Sundanese, and so he scribbled the name "Dayo" on his maps. And that's how the Portuguese would remember it for centuries thereafter.[13]

Meanwhile, the neighbouring kingdom of Demak started to plot its move to take Banten and Kelapa. This is when a general by the name of Fatahillah enters history. He is now considered one of Indonesia's national heroes and a kind of founding father of Jakarta. Little is known about this man and there is even some confusion about his name; sometimes he is referred to as Falatehan. But it appears he was born a common man in Pase in northern Sumatra and his father was an Arab from Gujarat.[14] At the time, Pase was a religious centre and it seems that this somehow rubbed off on Fatahillah because he travelled to the city of Mecca to study Islam for a few years. When a few years later Fatahillah returned from Mecca, he showed up in the Muslim port town of Jepara in Java, not far from Demak.

The king of Demak was interested in this fresh arrival from Mecca and Fatahillah must have impressed the king with his military skills as he was given the task of conquering Banten. Fatahillah promptly set off with an army and, after a short military incursion, succeeded in getting Banten to submit to Demak. His next stop was Kelapa, which he also conquered.

One of the first things he did there was to kick the Portuguese out of town and change the name of the town from Kelapa to Jayakarta – "the victorious city". The exact date of this victory and the proclamation of the new name is lost to history but some historians say – although with little evidence to show for it – that this all happened on 22 June 1527, now the official birthday of the city of Jakarta. We now also find the first mention of the name "Jakarta", written down a few decades after Fatahillah's victory by Portuguese historian João de Barros. In 1552, he refers to the city "Xacatara".

In the late sixteenth century, a new set of European explorers sailed into the seas near Jayakarta. Sir Francis Drake was the first Englishman to arrive in the archipelago when he circumnavigated the world from 1577 to 1580. At the time, cloves were one of the prized spices that the English, like the Dutch, wanted to get access to. When the English arrived in Jayakarta, they set up a lodge on the western side of the Ciliwung river in north Jayakarta.

The first Dutch ships arrived in 1596 under the command of Cornelis de Houtman. By 1611, the Dutch had agreed with the Muslim prince of Jayakarta, Pangeran Wijayakrama, to set up warehouses on the eastern side of the Ciliwung River, facing their English adversaries on the opposite bank. The Dutch named these newly constructed storerooms Nassau and Mauritius.

But building warehouses on the soggy soil proved to be a challenge and the Nassau started to sink into the swampy foundation. Another problem was the risk of supplies going up in smoke as fires were a regular occurrence in the densely packed city. It was decided that the walls would be constructed with stone and, to reduce risk further, the Dutch negotiated the demolition of wooden Chinese houses adjacent to the Nassau and Mauritius warehouses.

****

By now, these two countries had set up companies to spearhead the profitable trade in spices. The Dutch named theirs the Vereenigde Oostindische Compagnie (Dutch East India Company), abbreviated to

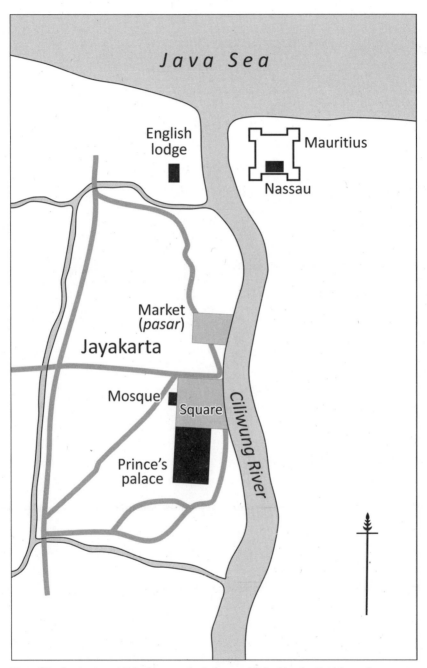

Map of Jayakarta circa 1618, showing the lodge established by the British on the western bank of the Ciliwung River, facing the Dutch warehouses Mauritius and Nassau on the eastern bank. The location of the Prince's palace roughly corresponds to the location of the current Mercure Jakarta Batavia hotel in Kota, north Jakarta.

VOC; even today it is still referred to by Indonesians as the *kompeni*. The English equivalent was the East India Company. The operations of the VOC were governed by a board of seventeen gentlemen running the operations from Amsterdam. The Heeren Zeventien were powerful, but the day-to-day operations in Batavia were managed by a Governor-General. He and his local council ran a private company that acted as a quasi-sovereign which could issue legislation and decide on matters concerning the law.

This is where Jan Pietersz Coen enters the scene. This controversial figure is seen by some as a visionary who kick-started the rise of a Dutch colonial empire, while others consider him a murderous psychopath. The less flattering reputation was earned in 1621, when he ordered a genocidal mission to the island of Banda, one of the original Spice Islands where nutmeg and cloves were sourced. In a matter of days, the Dutch violently reduced the number of Bandanese from 14,000 to only 480 with the help of Japanese samurai, Dutch soldiers and a few Javanese prisoners willing to provide a helping hand.

After setting up camp in Jayakarta, Dutch trade flourished and the VOC needed more than the two small warehouses for storage. What they wanted was a proper headquarters in Asia, preferably an easily defendable fort, that would help coordinate their trade across the archipelago. Jayakarta – they called it "Jacatra" – offered a number of advantages, such as proximity to a narrow sea lane – the Sunda Strait – where Dutch ships entered the archipelago from the Indian Ocean.

Jayakarta was at the time under control of the city of Banten, which had increased tariffs, much to the displeasure of Coen, at the time the second-ranked man for the VOC in the archipelago. Eventually, it was decided that Jayakarta was the perfect place to establish a regional headquarters for the Dutch. The local prince of Jayakarta was initially open to the idea, hoping to grow rich from all the new trade that had come to his city. In addition, he thought these new Dutch friends with guns could prove be useful. It was likely that he was hoping to establish an independent kingdom with the help of Dutch guns.

Thus, by 1618, a number of competing interests had their eyes on Jayakarta. First, there was the city of Jayakarta and its ambitious prince. Then there was Demak, located to the east of Jayakarta and in control of the city after Fatahillah conquered it. The growing empire of Mataram, much further away in Central Java, was also starting to show an interest. Add to this the Dutch, who at the time were keen on using Jayakarta as a trading base but had intentions to control the city, and lastly the English, who had a small presence in town and were eager to see the Dutch leave. With so many suitors, things were bound to go horribly wrong for Jayakarta.

Tensions rose when Coen ordered soldiers to fortify the warehouses. The prince of Jayakarta considered this an act of defiance and started to erect his own fortifications. It was the English who lit the match that finally set off this geopolitical powder keg. On 14 December 1618, the English seized a Dutch ship. Upon hearing the news, Coen promptly ordered his men to burn down the English lodge on the opposite bank of the river.[15] Matters rapidly spun out of control. The English sought to retaliate and the time seemed ripe when the arrival of several English ships meant they outnumbered the Dutch. Coen set off for the Moluccas – the group of islands at the centre of the spice trade – in search of Dutch reinforcements. But that meant leaving the Dutch behind at the mercy of the English.

Or so they thought. While the English were preparing an attack, troops from Banten arrived. The last thing its leader, Arya Ranamanggala, wanted was for the English to take control over Jayakarta after the Dutch were kicked out.[16] Thus, instead of allowing the English to attack the Dutch, he started to wrangle with the English over future power arrangements and eventually drove the English out. By then, the English had decided that India might be a more suitable place for its colonial ambitions; it would be a few centuries before they returned to Java. The Banten forces also gave chase to the Jayakarta ruler, who fled to the mountains. Banten was now in control of the city.

Meanwhile, the Dutch were holed up in their small fort and their warehouses. Realising they had avoided immediate annihilation, they decided to celebrate the delay of the attack by consuming copious amounts of beer and rice wine. There was even more cause for celebration when news arrived that Dutch ships had been spotted in the seas north of the city. On 28 May 1619, Coen stepped ashore with reinforcements from the Moluccas. He was not in the mood for negotiations and promptly burnt the whole town of Jayakarta to the ground. After chasing Bantenese forces away he proclaimed the founding of a new city with the name "Batavia", a reference to an ancient Germanic tribe.

The Dutch were now fully in control of the city for the first time. It was not for three centuries that the names "Jayakarta" or "Jacatra" would be used again.

Chapter 2
Trijntje and Souw Beng Kong
1619–1650

In the 1600s, the Dutch, English, and Portuguese were shipping administrators, soldiers, traders and all kinds of other folk, who had come from Europe to Southeast Asia in order to control as much as possible of the lucrative spice trade. The stakes were high as spices, such as nutmeg and cloves, fetched exorbitant prices in Europe, where they were used as preservatives and flavourings.

The lives of some of these people can be traced through ship records, church archives and, more extensively, through the diligent scribblings of the staff who recorded the court proceedings of the day. These records provide a treasure trove of information about what people did, where they lived, who they married and, obviously, why they were in court. This is how we make the acquaintance of a young lady by the name of Trijntje Willemsd.[1]

In December 1621, Trijntje left her hometown of Amersfoort and made her way a few hundred kilometres north to Texel, the first and largest of a chain of islands strung across the northern part of the Netherlands. It was a dark, windy, cold and rainy afternoon when she arrived in Texel to sign up for the long voyage to the sun-baked shores of Batavia. A little further from the registration office was her mode of transport, the *Walcheren*.

For reasons unknown, the young widow had decided to seek her fortune in a new city on the other side of the world. At the time in Batavia, there were very few Dutch women compared to men, so single women who arrived had a good chance of picking up husbands with substantially better social standing and larger wallets than they could hope for back in Holland. Perhaps this was on her mind when she stepped aboard the ship that cold December day. Indeed, once at sea she soon met a man called Floris Hendricksz and they would marry a few months later in Batavia.

Records[2] show that the *Walcheren* made swift progress on the way to Cape Town, where it stocked up with supplies. It then circumnavigated the treacherous waters around the Cape, boosted by the winter monsoon on the Indian Ocean typical for that time of the year, and reached the port of Batavia in just over five months, dropping anchor on 27 May 1622. Dutch ships were quite large, so the *Walcheren* waited in deeper water offshore while smaller boats, owned and crewed by locals, sailed out to ferry passengers and cargo to the port. In the distance she would have seen the coast lined with the lanky palm trees the port was famous for. The painting on the previous spread, *View of Batavia* by Hendrick Dubbels, gives an idea of Trijntje's first sight of Batavia as she was ferried in. By then the city had already expanded to the right of the river entrance. This would also be the first time Trijntje made contact with local workers, who were busy moving the goods into the smaller, lighter ferry boats.

Trijntje arrived in a busy town that was in the middle of a construction boom. As she stepped ashore, she would have encountered horse-drawn wagons filled with local coral and workmen stacking logs from the surrounding areas near the Ciliwung into large piles. Houses had been built here and there and wooden shops with thatched roofs were on both sides of the river. But the biggest real estate project in town was the construction of a large castle. Trijntje could not miss it – it was right opposite where her ferry moored. Three years before she arrived, the first warehouses that the

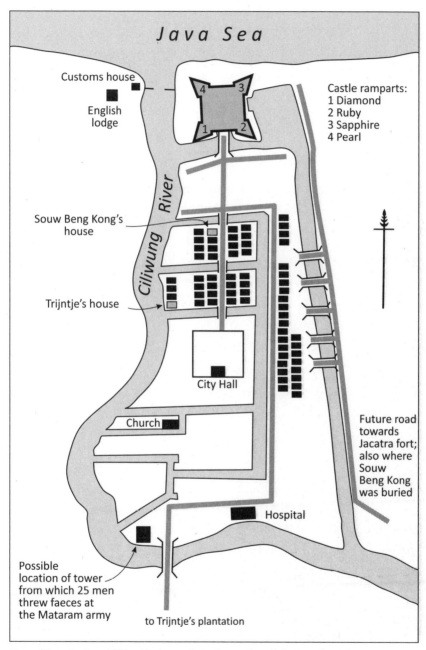

Map of Batavia circa 1628 with the castle in the north and the city along the eastern bank of the Ciliwung river, where Trijntje's house and the City Hall were also located.

Dutch had built, the Nassau and the Mauritius, were torn down to make way for this ambitious project. The castle was right on the seashore, so the northern ramparts could be used to defend any attack from naval forces.

After registration, the next challenge she faced was navigating the muddy streets leading into the city. This gave her a clear view of the castle's southern ramparts, the city's last line of defence against invaders from the sea. The castle was to be, quite literally, the city's crown jewel: the northern ramparts were called Pearl and Sapphire, and the bigger, more important south-facing ramparts, Ruby and Diamond. The names stuck. Even now, centuries later, some people still refer to that section of northern Jakarta near where the castle was built as *Kota Intan* ("precious city"). Nothing is left of this castle today but its most southern location was near where the railway now crosses Jl. Cengkeh (Clove Street) in Kota.

Planning a castle is one thing; building one, thousands of miles from home, with no adequate equipment in swampy ground is altogether a very different challenge. The local population was not going to offer much support – after all, the Dutch had just burned down their city. But, for a decent fee, some cash-strapped local workers, a large contingent of Chinese labourers, and other settlers who had made Batavia home were willing to offer the VOC a helping hand.

In front of the fort was a market that provided food as well as shelter against the midday heat. The biggest challenge during construction was the soggy ground on which the castle's foundations were built. The Ruby rampart soon sank into the swampy soil. A few years later, the two northern ramparts suffered a similar fate, and needed to be rebuilt. But eventually, the castle started to take shape.[3]

Within a stone's throw of the castle a small town started to appear. The initial idea was to follow the Dutch tradition of city planning. Three small tributaries that flowed into the Ciliwung river were straightened and deepened. The soil from the canals was used to raise the level of land in between the canals and this is where houses, churches and a city hall were constructed. The first three east-west canals were, in time, named the Amsterdamse gracht (Amsterdam Canal), the Groenegracht (Green Canal) and the Leeuwinnengracht (Lioness Canal).[4] A few decades later, the Groenegracht was filled in to make space for houses and a church. Later, a little further south from these three canals, a fourth east-west canal was dug. To square the new canals off, a north-south canal perpendicular to these three was created. This was called Tijgergracht (Tiger Canal), and is today Jl. Pos, a congested street. A large gate bearing its name is still visible beside a Daihatsu dealership.

The result of all the digging was a neat rectangular canal grid – the eastern grid of the city – along which houses, schools and a church could be built. This small town was protected to the west and the south by the Ciliwung River, to the north by the castle and to round it off, another larger canal was dug from the moat of the castle to a bend in the river. The whole town was now protected by water. Tijgergracht, in particular, developed into a beauty, lined with coconut and tamarind trees and elegant Dutch houses with large stoops. There, people sat in the evenings to smoke pipes and chat with neighbours. Small boats would carry some of the newly arrived goods across the canals to nearby warehouses. Hawkers would roam the streets selling snacks, *sateh* and fish. Tijgergracht soon became Batavia's prime residential address.

Another example of the Dutch approach to town planning was the erection of a town hall right in the middle of this grid, although it took a few decades and multiple alterations before it was eventually finished in 1710.[5] The City Hall still stands there today, proudly towering over Fatahillah Square. Today, it the home of the Jakarta History Museum. From City Hall, Prinsenstraat ran straight north to the entrance of the castle. The street is still there, but is now called Jl. Cengkeh.

JAKARTA

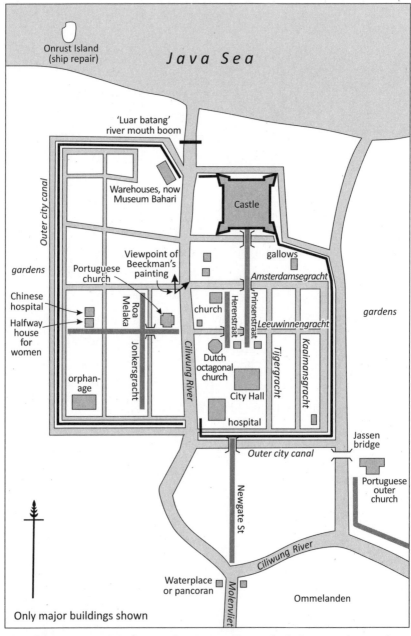

Map of Batavia circa 1650, showing the city extending on both the east and west sides of the Ciliwung river. In the centre is where Beeckman sat to make his painting (see pages 48–49) and further south, outside the city, the Pancoran (see page 65) and the end of the Molenvliet canal.

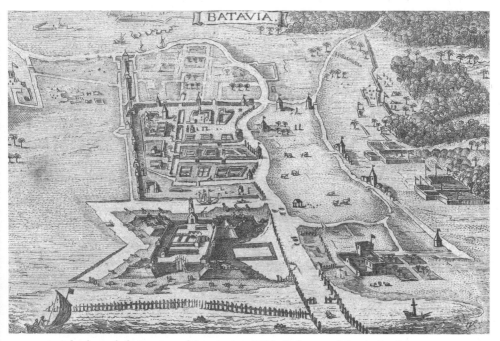

An inland, south-facing view of Batavia circa 1629. Only part of the city has been constructed at this point, just south of the castle, with City Hall and Tijgergracht (on left of picture) completed.

****

Trijntje was swallowed up by this town and would have been lost to history but for an entry in the city archives that mentions her name a month after she arrived. This records her marriage to Floris Hendricksz, and permission for their marriage was granted by the governor, Jan Pietersz Coen. She declared that her husband in the Netherlands had passed away, and she was allowed to remarry. Her marital status was of no particular concern to Coen, who was eager to grow Batavia into a centre of commerce and wanted more women like Trijntje to come and populate his fast-growing city.

Trijntje and Floris were able to get a house right on the river along the Leeuwinnengracht, just a block away from where City Hall was under construction. Her garden would border a small bend in the Ciliwung

River from where she might have seen the remnants of the old English lodge, burned down a few years earlier.

Someone looking at the Dutch-style houses neatly arranged along the canals would have had the impression that Batavia was a Dutch city. But Trijntje would have noted the large number of Chinese walking around the streets and working on the construction sites. The Chinese, in fact, far outnumbered the Dutch. Francois Valentijn, the Dutch explorer, naturalist, preacher and author would write in his magnus opus, *Old and New East Indies*, a century later that "without the Chinese, Batavia would be nothing".[6]

Later on, Trijntje and Floris found a small stretch of swampy land just a little further south, on the opposite, west bank of the Ciliwung. There, they successfully converted a soggy marsh into a neat, small plantation with a few hundred coconut, lemon, orange, and banana trees. The fruit was probably sold at the market opposite the castle. For this young couple, it proved to be a prosperous enterprise as Trijntje and Floris managed twenty slaves, mostly native Indonesians, on the plantations and eventually, the two of them were able to make enough money to construct a large stone house. After some time they also started a much more profitable business: turning the sap of the palm tree into *tuak* (fermented palm wine) and selling it to the local taverns.

For Trijntje, daily life started early. Most days, she woke up well before dawn. Carpenters and other construction workers started their first shift at six in the morning and from where Trijntje lived, she would have seen many of them walk towards the castle or along the canals in the cool dawn. For breakfast, they would have some watery rice gruel with dried fish. By then, she would have chewed her first *sirih* (betel nut) of the day. Her neighbour had warned her about eating rice in the morning – it was said to cause blindness – but the doctor had assured her that regular portions of raw shark liver would ward off this particular affliction.

An artist's impression of daily life in Batavia in the late 1620s, showing the market square with an early version of the town hall in the background.

Then she would join her husband to inspect their coconut and fruit plantations just outside the town. On the way to the plantation, along the Leeuwinnengracht, she would pass a Chinese tea shop that at that time of the day would have just opened its doors to carpenters who started their daily routine with a morning smoke and a cup of tea. Others would chew their first *sirih* of the day. She would turn right, pass an open area with the City Hall on her left. Accompanied by children walking to a nearby school, she would cross a bridge and enter the land surrounding the city. By 1631, a new large gate was built and simply named Nieuwpoort (New Gate).

After the inspection of the plantations and taking care of her *tuak* business, she would make her way back to town along the same road, crossing the river via the bridge and passing the teahouses to eventually arrive at the market near the castle on the opposite side of town. Walking there, she would carry her small umbrella or *payung* to shield herself against the increasingly ferocious sun.

Making her rounds at the market, Trijntje would see a wide variety of local produce – beetroot, radish, carrots, long beans, and cabbage – harvested from some of the gardens of the local houses. Rice was cultivated in small paddy fields outside the city walls, but was also shipped in by Mataram traders from the north coast of Java. The best time to buy rice was when fully loaded ships arrived, which meant prices were lower for a few days. Fish was also widely available, while the supply of game was determined by the success of hunting parties that had returned from nearby forests. Sometimes, exotic delicacies made their way to the market, as was the case when soldiers caught a crocodile in one of the canals.

Later in the day, Trijntje would mend shoes and clothing at home and, after a nap to avoid the midday heat, perhaps go visit friends or stroll along the beautiful Tijgergracht in the cool afternoon. On Sundays, she would dress up and join the rest of the town at the Dutch Reformed Church, something we know she did for certain as her name is in the church archives. Afterwards, she would sometimes visit a friend's house to enjoy refreshments such as Spanish wine or chew *sirih*. By nine in the evening, she was ready to go to bed.

A few years later, in 1625, Trijntje faced her first major setback when Floris passed away. She now had to manage the whole business on her own. Meanwhile, city builder and governor Coen had problems of his own: he was having trouble paying all the workers and suppliers of the stones and wood that he had bought for construction. Coen repeatedly mailed letters to the VOC headquarters in Amsterdam to ask for more funding. But Coen was not a diplomat; in the same letter in which he asks his bosses, the council of seventeen that managed the VOC, for money, he also accuses them of being narrow-minded and stupid for failing to provide him with the funds earlier. At times he even had to borrow from the sailors. Still, using whatever money he was able to get his hands on, good progress was made. A new hospital was erected in the southern edge of the rectangular grid, adjacent to the local cemetery and not far from Trijntje's house. She would pass it on the way to her plantation. But by the time a school was constructed, Coen ran out of money. A creative mind suggested organising a city lottery, perhaps as a means to attract money from the well-off Chinese community. This must have done the trick because on a map from 1627 we find evidence of a school, made of stone, right in the middle of the city.

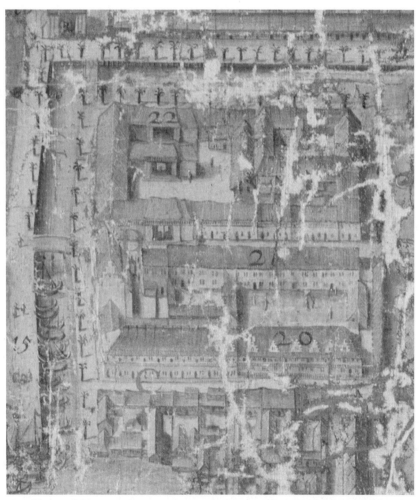

The oldest available map of Batavia, dating to 1627, shows a school (numbered 20 on the image) "located at the north end of the Herenstraat, on the east side; behind it a square that extended to the 'Vrouwenhof' located on the westside of Prinsenstraat" [author's translation from De Haan, vol. 1, p. 51]. The map is from the collection of Westfries Museum and can be viewed in its entirety on the museum's website.

At the corner of the Amsterdamse gracht and Prinsenstraat, near the castle, lived Souw Beng Kong, also known as "Bencon", the first Kapitein (captain) of the Chinese community.[7] In his 16 years in this position he played an important role in consolidating Dutch rule in Batavia by encouraging the settlement of Chinese migrants, starting with 170 Chinese families that left Banten to set up shop in Batavia. Strictly speaking, these Chinese families identified as Peranakan. Prior to the late nineteenth century, Chinese immigrants were all male because Chinese women were not allowed to leave the country. As a result the men who came from China married the local Javanese women, and their progeny was known as Peranakan. The Peranakan term *nyonya* – meaning "female" and now widely referring to local women married to Chinese men in Indonesia – comes from Hokkien, a Chinese dialect that many Chinese immigrants spoke.

Coen understood the importance of these Chinese traders and was eager to keep good relations with them. In those days, the VOC left each ethic group to handle their own internal issues unless matters spilled over onto the broader community. This was pretty much the common practice in many trading hubs across Asia in those days. But for the Chinese, a special position was created when Coen allowed their Kapitein to sit on the judicial council of Batavia. This position almost certainly helped Souw Beng Kong to build a commercial empire. His legal and political powers grew until 1624 when the council decided that he could no longer impose the death penalty on his business adversaries.[8]

The role of the Kapitein was not just to protect and rule his community, he was also an unofficial representative for the Dutch authorities. Chinese travellers or traders who arrived in Batavia by boat were asked to report to the Kapitein of the Chinese first, who would then issue a permit for them to engage in their business. This must have been profitable as Souw Beng Kong eventually settled in a grand residence outside the city at Mangga

Dua, where Coen had given him some land. To make sure everyone knew of his importance, a banner outside his country estate read "the original founder of this region". He was buried there and his grave is one of Batavia's oldest landmarks, these days located in a small alley off Jl. Pangeran Jayakarta that still carries his name.

****

If you build it they will come, as the saying goes. The city grew fast. In 1619, Coen estimated that some 2,000 people were living in Batavia; by 1624, this had grown to 8,000.[9] But in the eyes of Coen, most of the people coming from Holland were a bunch of crooked, lazy sailors with an unhealthy interest in alcohol and women. In his letters to the VOC headquarters he complained that only the "scum of the earth" arrived in his town. He probably had a point. Harbour towns and garrisons were typically cesspits of vice and Batavia was no exception. In the early days, Batavia was a male enclave where sailors and other VOC employees gambled away their money, ran up debts, and got involved with fights, while indulgence in prostitution and adultery allowed for the rampant spread of sexually transmitted diseases.

Coen wanted a population policy which would encourage the "right" type of people to come and set up shop in Batavia, such as Trijntje and Floris for example, who had helped build the community. Coen himself lead by example. On a trip back to report to the VOC headquarters in Amsterdam, he married Eva Ment and took her, her brother and a sister, back to Batavia.

Around this time, another man from Holland, Justus Heurnius, arrived in Batavia. Heurnius was a well-educated Dutchman who had studied theology and medicine in Leiden before he decided to sail east. He arrived two years after Trijntje, in 1624, and enthusiastically started to work on building what would become Batavia's first church community. At the time there were some Sunday services organised by a handful of people, but Heurnius gave the Christian community more structure. He also learned Chinese and Malay and created the first Dutch-Latin-Chinese dictionary.

As pastor-in-chief, Heurnius worked with a half-Portuguese, half-Bandanese pastor by the name of Cornelis Senen, who had arrived in town a few years earlier. The newcomer was from Banda, one of the original Spice Islands, where Jan Pietersz Coen had massacred the population in 1621. In Batavia, Cornelis Senen became chief of the Bandanese community, active in the church and a school, and preached in Malay. However, lacking any Dutch blood in his veins, he was never accepted as a full pastor by the Batavian church. Heurnius got on very well with this multi-talented man who over time became a bit of a local celebrity. He was admired by many and was called "Teacher Cornelis" or, in Dutch, "Meester Cornelis". Locals just called him "Mester".

Meester Cornelis had a good eye for worldly investments. He acquired a house on the fancy Tijgergracht and much later bought land some twelve kilometres south of Batavia, near the Ciliwung River. That gave him access to a forest; the logged timber was thrown into the river for easy transport to Batavia and sold to local construction workers and carpenters. To protect the loggers and workers from the guerrillas of Mataram and Banten, their houses were surrounded by a thorny bamboo fence. This fence gave its name to the *kampung* it surrounded, an area still known as Bukit Duri or "thorny hill".[10] Slowly, all this land near the river came to be known simply as Meester Cornelis. The name stuck and it was not until four centuries later that the name changed to Jatinegara although, even today, locals still call the district "Mester".

****

Batavia was now growing fast, a fact that did not go unnoticed in the Mataram Sultanate in central Java. The view was that something needed to be done to nip this new city in the bud as soon as possible. On 22 August 1628, some 60 ships manned by 900 Mataram warriors arrived at the mouth of the Ciliwung, asking for access to Batavia. "We come in peace," was their message. But the astute governor Coen smelled a rat and let only 20 ships in. Unknown to him, they were part of a master plan – a large Mataram army was poised to attack the city from the south.[11]

The problem was that the army came two days late. This was unknown to the Mataram boatmen, who attacked the castle on a pre-determined date at midnight under the assumption they would get support from the Mataram army. One group made their way up the Diamond and Ruby ramparts while others attacked the northern side of the castle at Pearl. But Dutch troops beat off the initial attack. The Mataram warriors, lacking support from the army, had no choice but to run back to their boats and sail off.

Forewarned, the Batavians had time to regroup. Two days later they found a large army camping outside the southern gates of the city. While preparing to attack, the advancing soldiers noted the reddish colour of the soil – red earth is *tanah abang* in Javanese – and the name stuck; hence, the modern Jakarta city district of Tanah Abang.

Meanwhile, Coen ordered all people south of the fourth canal to retreat to the castle, where it was easiest to defend against an attack. The Mataram army entered the southern parts of the city where a church and several houses were burnt down, including Trijntje's residence near the river. At the same time, part of the army moved to the western bank of the river and cut down all the trees on Trijntje's plantation. She lost everything she had worked for.

But while the marauding Mataram army was able to cause a serious amount of damage it did not penetrate the towers on the southern city wall. One tower, Hollandia, was defended by 25 men who rained uninterrupted fire on the Mataram attackers below as the entrance could only be reached by ladder.

The Mataram rushed to put up ladders but these were easily pushed back. They threw spears and rocks and even tried to smoke the Batavians out. Nothing worked. Re-assessing their strategy, they decided to attack the towers on the night of 21 September 1628, around a month after the arrival of the naval flotilla. The Mataram now had an advantage. The men holed up in the tower had run out of food and bullets. Their situation looked dire. The only available weapons were clay pots filled with faeces which they threw over the walls. That seems to have done the job as the disgusted Mataram troops left the towers alone. For a long time after, this part of town was somewhat jokingly referred to as *kota thai* ("shit town").[12]

While reeking clay pots might have saved the day, that wasn't the real problem facing Mataram army commanders. The real issue was that they too had run out of food. This did not go unnoticed by the Dutch soldiers still holed up in the tower. One of them, Hans Madelijn, was hoisted down from the tower in the middle of the night and ran to the castle a few hundred meters away to report the news. Governor Coen decided that this was the opportune time for a counter-attack.

It worked. The hungry Mataram army retreated and for the moment, peace and quiet returned to whatever was left of the city. But this was no time to celebrate a victory as governor Coen suspected the Mataram army had not given up. He ordered the construction of more towers on the western side of the city wall and burned rice paddy fields outside the walls to make sure food was in short supply.

Coen was right. A few months later, on 21 August 1629, a new Mataram army arrived at the city wall with a different strategy. This time, they threw large numbers of dead bodies in the Ciliwung to poison

Batavia's water supply. But the burned paddy fields meant they too faced food shortages and by October they had to retreat. Shortly after their departure, Coen died from disease, perhaps because of the contaminated river water. He was buried in the only cemetery in Batavia at the time, and his grave was later transferred to a church, although, to this day, its exact location remains unknown.

****

Meanwhile, as intermittent waves of Mataram attacks pounded the city walls for two years, a new tragedy unfolded right in the middle of Batavia.[13] Taking centre stage was 13-year-old Sara Specx, half-Dutch and half-Japanese, the bastard daughter of Jacques Specx, a senior officer in the VOC and a future governor of Batavia.

Specx knew Coen quite well, as colleagues of the VOC. Thus, when Specx was ordered by the VOC back to headquarters in Amsterdam, he decided to leave his daughter Sara in Batavia under the care of the Coen family. Coen's wife, Eva Ment, had several young ladies under her wing and they all lived at the castle.

In June 1629, about a year after Sara's father left, Coen's household became the setting of a major scandal. Pieter Cortenhoef, a 16-year-old ensign working for the VOC, had become an admirer of Sara and it appears that the feeling was mutual. The court filings tell us that one afternoon, Pieter made his way to Sara's room where she had prepared a mat on the floor to allow Pieter, to do "twice, whatever he wanted".

Coen, it is recorded, flew into a terrible fury when he heard the news. The same man who had complained to his bosses in Amsterdam about the immorality of many of his fellow "scum of the earth" countrymen, now faced an embarrassing scandal in his own household. To Coen the case was clear — both had to be put to death, preferably immediately.

Preacher Heurnius arrived in time to persuade Coen against such a rash decision. Proper procedures needed to be followed. Heurnius and others also argued that Sara was too young to understand the consequences of her actions.

Sara and Pieter were put in jail for the night so that the Council of Judges could convene. But the next morning Coen made it very clear to the judges that the rules of the VOC were quite clear on this matter – pre-marital sex was punishable by death.

A majority of the council ruled that Pieter was to be decapitated and Sara was to be put in a barrel and thrown into the river. Only one of the members of the council, future governor Antonio van Diemen, refused to sign this order. But it then occurred to Preacher Heurnius that life sentences could only be imposed on people over 14 years of age. So, instead of being drowned, she was whipped in the town hall, with all doors open so that the whole town could hear her screams. Trijntje lived nearby and must have heard poor young Sara.

****

We pick up the trail of Trijntje again in a letter to the government.[14] After the death of her husband Floris and losing her house and plantations to the plundering Mataram army, Trijntje wanted to marry again. But gossip around town had it that her first husband in the Netherlands was not dead at all. She had simply run away from a bad marriage and landed in Batavia. True or not, these rumours had an effect and the local church council rejected her request to remarry.

But Trijntje did not give up. She put her case to the government in an appeal dated 1 February 1631 in which we learn how Trijntje picked up her life after losing her husband and all her possessions in the Mataram attacks. To make some money, she first distilled *arak* (rice wine), then set up a brickyard and later tried her luck with growing trees in a small garden. These enterprises flourished and soon this entrepreneurial woman erected a new brick house, a "jewel for the city" in her view. Being such a good citizen, she argued, surely the government would allow her to remarry.

Given the VOC's apparent desire to encourage more women to settle down and prosper in the city, Trijntje must have been very disappointed when her request was denied. There is a court record that showed that Trijntje, presumably frustrated with the situation, later had a few run-ins with the police.

After Coen's death and the retreat of the Mataram army, the recently returned Jacques Specx was reunited with his humiliated daughter and appointed as the new governor. He, together with Coen and his successor, Antonio van Diemen, were the three great builders of Batavia. In Specx's time, the eastern grid of canals was expanded. One ran parallel to the Tijgergracht and was named Kaaimansgracht (Crocodile Canal). The southern area surrounding this canal was where the Bandanese community settled and was aptly named the Bandanese quarter. This is where Meester Cornelis was active and covers roughly the area where the Museum Bank Negara Indonesia (BNI) now stands.

Specx also gave orders to build walls on the southern and eastern sides of the city to ensure that it was better protected against any future Mataram attack. A new large bridge on the southern side was built with a big gate in front of it. This was Nieuwpoort (New Gate) and a street extended south beyond the city to an area filled with Chinese houses, vegetable gardens and plantations. The name given to that street is still in use today – Jl. Pintu Besar, or "large gate street" in Malay.

The eastern grid of the city was now finished. It was time for a similar mirror-image grid to be built on the opposite bank of the Ciliwung; that work was completed when Antonio van Diemen was governor. It was he who tasked a sailor, Abel Tasman, to explore some of the unknown lands and seas south of Java. In 1642, Tasman became the first European to step ashore an island that he named Van Dieman's Land in honour of the governor. It is now named after him – Tasmania.

The western side of the city was originally dominated by a shipyard facing the Diamond rampart of the castle on the other side of the Ciliwung (major ship repairs were done on a nearby island called Onrust). The small shipyard was where the English lodge used to be, an area currently located between Jl. Kakap and the Kali Besar. Van Diemen constructed new city walls on the western side and a lookout tower, built much later in 1839, is still there. Within these new walls large warehouses stored cloves, cotton and coffee. These *westzijdse pakhuizen* ("western warehouses") are still very much worth a visit and now host the Museum Bahari. Outside the walls is a *kampung* called Luar Batang ("outside log"), a reference to a large log used by customs officers to close off the river in the evening.[15] The *kampung* still stands today.

Having established new walls and warehouses, Van Diemen pretty much replicated the rectangular canal grid seen on the opposite side of the river. Almost a mirror image to the Tijgergracht on the east side, a main canal was dug in 1637 to act as the main north-south axis. This was Jonkersgracht (Jonker's Canal). In a southwestern corner of this grid we find the *spin huis* (a correctional facility for women) and an orphanage. Today a noodle shop, Orpa, reminds us of the orphanage's location. A nearby bridge provided access to the west of this grid, where vegetable gardens were kept and cows grazed. This bridge crossing the river was at the end of Utrechtstreet (Jl. Kopi today) and is, in a different form, still there.

Having rebuilt the city of Batavia, it was time for grander schemes. Several times in the past the VOC had attempted to take over the Portuguese regional stronghold of Malacca, northwest of Batavia on the

Malay peninsula, without success. Malacca, defended by an impressive fortress, was important because it controlled access to the narrow sea lanes of the Straits of Malacca and the spice trade there. By 1638 the Dutch were preparing to try again and entered talks with the sultanate of Johor, a territory which was also eager to send the Portuguese packing.[16] With the condition that the Dutch would stay out of the rest of the Malay peninsula, the two forces jointly attacked the city of Malacca in 1640. After a siege of three months, the city defences broke in early January 1641 and Dutch and Johorean forces pillaged the city and burned large parts of it down. This effectively destroyed the Portuguese influence in the Malay region. The Dutch took control of Malacca and agreed not to seek any further territories or wage war with the Malay kingdoms.

After this conquest, a number of Portuguese from Malacca moved and settled in Batavia on a street that they named after their hometown – Jl. Roa Malaka – in the western part of the town, along the Jonkersgracht. A Portuguese church was built too.

The Dutch also sent a large trophy back from Malacca to Batavia: a giant cannon that carried the name Si Jagur, possibly a reference to its Macao-based manufacturer.[17] It was initially positioned at the entrance to the castle but over time was moved to the northern part of Fatahillah Square in front of the City Hall in old Batavia. It is not its weight or size of the cannon that became its trademark, but its breech: a *figa*, a fist with the thumb between the index and the middle fingers. This was a symbol for good luck but over time it turned into a fertility symbol – women who hoped to get pregnant came from all over to touch it. The cannon still stands there today.

This, then, is what Batavia looked like in the middle of the 1600s: like a butterfly, it had two large, near-identical rectangular wings with mirror-image canal grids and in the middle ran the Ciliwung River. Despite threats from the nearby Javanese kingdoms of Mataram and

Banten, it was a flourishing town. Around 1661, a talented painter, Andries Beeckman, set up his easel one day in a spot near the Ciliwung with a great view of the castle. Today, *The Castle of Batavia* (see previous spread) hangs at the Rijksmuseum in Amsterdam.

In Beeckman's work, the castle looks imposing. A small group of people are leaving through the castle gate, possibly the governor on his way to the town hall. In the foreground, on the western side of the river, we can see waving palm trees that shade a market where people of different races are rubbing shoulders with each other – in the foreground, a Dutch man is talking with a local woman under an umbrella carried by a slave, on the left, two Chinese (in long sleeves) are in conversation and in the background, a few local men are enjoying a ball game. Up in the palm trees are boys collecting coconuts to sell in the market. On the river, some boatmen are at work. The city painted by Beeckman is cosmopolitan, prosperous, peaceful and bustles with traders from different corners of the world.

Batavia continued to flourish and enjoy a period of peace and prosperity. A few decades later, in the early 1700s, the Dutch pastor-traveller Francois Valentijn visited Batavia and recorded that "the air is very fresh and healthy and the heat is not unbearable, but on the contrary, cool winds like one cannot believe it".[18] He also noted that crocodiles in the canals nourished themselves on "dead cats, dogs, buffalos and people that have been murdered".

By the time Andries Beeckman sat down to start his painting, most of the people we met in this chapter had moved on. The tortured Sara Specx eventually married and later moved to Formosa (present-day Taiwan), never to return to Batavia. There, she died at the young age of 19. When her father Jacques passed the governorship to his successor in 1632, the Chinese community showed their appreciation for his support and presented him with a gold medal engraved with a map

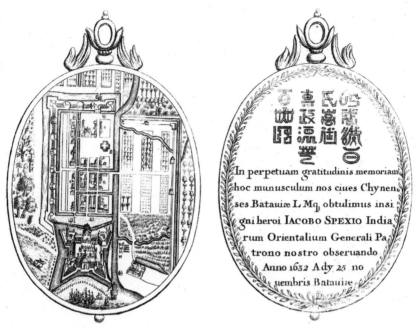

A medal presented to Jacques Specx by the members of the Chinese community in 1632 with an illustration of Batavia engraved on it. The church and square in front of City Hall are visible on the left side. The west (right) side of Batavia features gardens and small plantations enclosed by a wall and canal.

of Batavia. It is now on display at the Rijksmuseum in Amsterdam. In 1650, Jacques returned to Amsterdam.

The adventurous and bookish pastor Heurnius, one of the men who saved Sara from a much worse fate, travelled around several remote islands in the Indonesian archipelago before deciding to return to Holland where he and others took it upon themselves to translate the Bible into Malay. Heurnius passed away in 1652 in the small Dutch town of Wijk bij Duurstede.

On 7 April 1639 we find the last record of Trijntje. She died sixteen years after she arrived in Batavia on the *Walcheren*. Antonio van Diemen allowed her possessions to go to Dirk Pietersen van Maersen, manager of the horse stables of the VOC and the man with whom she seemingly spent the last years of her life.

The only one still wandering the streets of Batavia was Meester Cornelis who in 1656 had acquired a piece of land outside Batavia which would not only carry his name for centuries to come, but also point the direction of where the city's future lay.

This was to become known as the Ommelanden, or "the lands surrounding the city".

Chapter 3
Beyond the City Walls
1650–1700

By the 1650s, the fashionable thing for powerful European countries to do was to acquire colonies: the British decided to focus on India, the Dutch were in the Indonesian archipelago and the Spanish had a foothold in the Philippines. But it was not just domination in Asia that the Europeans wanted. All of them, especially the Spanish and Portuguese, were also looking to have a share of parts of the Americas. There, the Dutch had already established a settlement, New Amsterdam, at the southern tip of Manhatten Island. But in 1664, after much unrest and controversy, they surrendered it without a fight to the British, who renamed it New York.

In the last decades of the seventeenth century, this tussle for land and colonies amongst the European powers was to come to a head: the Dutch and the British were about to start a series of wars, and Portugal and Spain had a go at each other too. All this would have serious consequences for the city of Batavia.

****

In 1650, a Batavian administrator scribbled down the very first record of one of my ancestors. The archives show that a certain Barbara van der Linde, married to Pieter Nijdorp, arrived in the city the same year. The

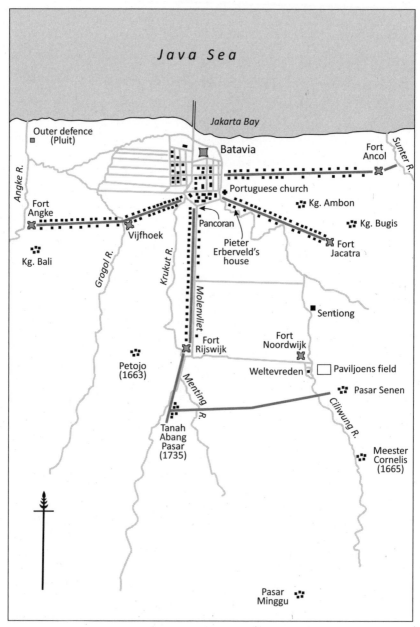

Batavia and the surrounding area, the Ommelanden, circa 1700. Canals connect the five defence forts. The outer defense (a fort called Pluit) is located in the north.

next record is of their daughter, Catherina Pieters van der Linde, who died as a widow in 1670. Interestingly, at the time of her death, Catherina went by Barbara's family name, not her father's, which might suggest she was raised by her mother. It seems Barbara also had a son, Jacob van der Linde, who married Elisabeth Laackeman from Amsterdam in December 1672 and was a junior merchant at the VOC. The last record of Barbara is in 1690, when church records show she attended the baptism of a baby girl. In 1702 her granddaughter was at a notary where an inheritance issue was discussed, possibly because Barbara had passed away.

We don't know what Barbara did, where she lived, what happened with her husband or exactly when she passed away. She just disappears from the archives. But we do know that Barbara would witness, in a span of about 50 years, the complete makeover of the lands surrounding Batavia. The so-called Ommelanden was transformed from a vulnerable backwater into one of the most densely populated rural areas in the Indonesian archipelago. This transformation dominated much of the social, political and economic life of late seventeenth-century Batavia and also formed the backdrop for Barbara's personal life.

The man who would play a major role in the transformation of the Ommelanden was a 17-year-old boy when he and his parents boarded a large yacht in December 1675, the *'t Huis te Kleef*,[1] at Texel in the Netherlands and bound for Batavia. Like so many other vessels, it would stop at Cape Town for about three weeks to undergo repairs and stock up on food. The journey across the Indian Ocean to Batavia took about eight months. The boy was called Cornelis Chastelein and, just like Trijntje and Barbara van der Linde before him, he would never return to Europe.[2]

The Chastelein family settled down and soon after that, young master Cornelis landed a job as a junior VOC bookkeeper at the castle. He lived in Batavia, eventually finding a house near the river on the west side of town near where, decades earlier, the palace of the Prince of Jayakarta was located – that is, before the Dutch burned it down. It is likely that Barbara van der Linde and her son Jacob, also employed by the VOC, had settled here too as this was where many new arrivals – including Cornelia van Rijn, the daughter of famous Dutch painter Rembrandt[3] – chose to stay in the second half of the seventeenth century.

To get to work at the castle in the morning, Cornelis would leave his house, cross the river by bridge or use the small boats that ferried people to the other side, turn left and make his way to a cow pasture, and then continue north across a canal and along streets lined with Chinese shophouses, teahouses and small restaurants. He would pass a small church and, upon approaching the castle, be met by the smell of fresh fruits, dried fish and vegetables coming from the market opposite the castle. In the distance, across the open land in front of the castle, Cornelis could sometimes see the gallows which, if there was a hanging, were typically in operation in the early morning.

As a bookkeeper, Cornelis would often travel between the castle on the east side of the city and the warehouses on the west bank of the river. There, he might have met Jacob van der Linde, the junior merchant and son of Barbara. For young men like Cornelis and Jacob with jobs of medium rank at the VOC, pay was notoriously low. It would have been hardly enough to get by on, let alone purchase a brick house along one of the canals. But in those days it was easy for an entrepreneurial employee of the *kompeni* to make some extra money. This was done through smuggling. Goods would be bought in Batavia, put on a VOC ship and, with the right payment to the captain, transported all the way to Amsterdam, where friends or family would pick up and sell them at a substantial profit.

Smuggling was rife and VOC officials at the docks in Amsterdam inspecting the unloading of goods from newly arrived ships from Batavia must have been aware of the amount of unregistered goods onboard. Still, it was condoned simply because everybody, including the inspectors, got a piece of the profits. Private trading schemes were also common on VOC ships heading for China, Japan or India and some men made so much money that they could afford to purchase their own ships to carry goods across Southeast Asia and China.

The preferred cargo ship of the day was called a *fluit*, Dutch for whistle, possibly a reference to their flat-bottomed design that allowed easy entry to shallow ports and rivers. Batavia's harbour had a whole fleet of these *fluit* ships; one was named *Het Witte Paert* ("the white horse"), constructed in Amsterdam in 1646. It carried cargo from Batavia to Japan, making stops in Taiwan. A common problem for these ships in Asia was the warm and humid tropical weather which cracked their curved planks. Perhaps this was the reason why by the late 1650s the *Het Witte Paert* was considered no longer seaworthy. Instead, its beams and masts were used to fortify a small outpost near the Angke estuary, west of Batavia, which handled sporadic attacks by marauding soldiers from the Banten kingdom. The fort was referred to as Fluit, a name that over time morphed into Pluit, now a district in north Jakarta.[4]

For a long time, nobody seemed to be bothered by all this smuggling and private trading. But by 1676, the VOC had had enough. The Heeren Zeventien, the executive board of the VOC, announced that all trade was to be done by the VOC alone and captains involved in these trading schemes were suspended. It had little effect. Multiple repeat announcements in the following years suggest that few heeded the warnings and continued with their private trading schemes. The profits involved were simply too attractive.

The irony was that the men who issued these orders were often the biggest smugglers of them all, allowing them to make fortunes in Batavia. Later, in the 1700s, even governors of Batavia were caught in the act. This is not a complete surprise as smuggling and trading were both much easier for those of high rank within the VOC hierarchy. A governor like

Jacob Mossel, who served from 1750 to 1761, earned 2,400 guilders a year. But with some risk taking and a bit of luck in smuggling, he was able to accumulate as much as 100,000 guilders a year. To many, the whole point of getting a promotion and moving up the VOC career ladder was to get better access to these money-making opportunities.[5] A particularly fast way up the ladder was to marry the daughter of a highly ranked VOC manager. Both Jacob van der Linde and Cornelis Chastelein adopted this strategy: Jacob married Elisabeth Laackeman, the widow of the chief surgeon at the VOC, and Cornelis wed Catherina of Quaelborg, the Indies-born daughter of a senior VOC councillor.

****

While all the smuggling and private trading schemes might have somewhat disadvantaged the VOC, it hugely benefitted the city of Batavia. The profits were spent at taverns and teahouses, and financed the construction of large brick houses, the acquisition of land for plantations, and the purchase of slaves. The profits were so substantial that by the 1680s the lifestyle of some Batavians were lavish, to say the least.

A letter written by a contemporary of Barbara van der Linde and Cornelis Chastelein provides a window into this life of luxury. Dated December 1689, it was written by a Cornelia Johanna van Beveren to her mother in Amsterdam.[6] Cornelia had a house on the Jonkersgracht (Jonker's Canal) in the west section of Batavia. This canal ran from the warehouses in the north to near the city wall in the south.

Cornelia writes that two months earlier she had got married to a certain Juriaen Beek. He was a "free burgher", which meant he had worked for the VOC and after his contract ended, decided to stay in Batavia to make a living. Cornelia is proud to relate that the wedding took two days and on each day, there were about eighty guests, "mostly young people". She continues with a detailed description of her bridal gown (black velvet with a train of about one-and-a-half metres long), her under gown (white satin and diamond buttons), her jewellery (pearls and a crown of mother-of-pearl and diamonds), the cushions in the church (green velvet) and the colour of the walls of her bridal apartment (also green).

She informs her mother that eight of her fifty-nine slaves are still children. She goes on to explain what they do:

> Three or four boys walk behind me and my husband when we go out and there are five or six boys and girls that stand behind us when we are at table, three boys that play bass, violin and harp when we are at the table. The rest of the boys I use for work at home, groceries, sewing and such kind of work; one takes care of the wine cellar, two or three in the kitchen so that each has their own work. The girls I use for sewing and linen work, three or four take care of me and one sits in the first room of the house to take the groceries [...] you now have heard the short description of the lives of the slaves.[7]

Cornelia's lavish lifestyle was not an exception. Batavia was a money magnet and everybody wanted a piece of the pie. No wonder that a large number of people flocked to the young city and, over time, it grew into a densely packed place. Houses were now built in rows along the canals and the risk of fire was something that the city administration could no longer ignore. At one point, one of the regular fires in the city destroyed many Chinese cottages built of wood and bamboo in the eastern part of Batavia. After another great fire swept through part of the western quarter, the Batavia government decreed in the 1660s that no more bamboo dwellings would be permitted in the city. While this prevented the spread of fire, a consequence was that poor people who could not afford a brick house had to settle outside the city walls. They moved into the lands surrounding the city, the Ommelanden.[8]

In those days it was not safe to spend time beyond the city walls. Dense and lush tropical forests surrounded the city, providing cover to marauding Banten soldiers, runaway slaves and other lowlifes. If that was not enough, rhinos, tigers and crocodiles roamed the area, happy to feed on inattentive visitors to the jungle.

By the time Barbara arrived in town, part of the forest was already being cleared for houses, gardens, and plantations. One of the first areas to be cleared was adjacent to the eastern part of the city, Kampung Muka, where the city organised an annual mango feast for orphans. On the south side of the city, the forest was cleared so cattle could graze. Even in those days it was referred to as Pinangsia ("cow street"), a name still in use today.

But in 1656 those that ventured outside the city wall were reminded how dangerous it was after a new conflict broke out between the VOC and Banten. A group of Banten soldiers plundered the area and burned down sugar mills and houses located some distance from the city. The VOC came to two realisations: one, that the Ommelanden had to be secure in order to facilitate the growth of the city, and two, they had to come to some agreement with the two empires that were the biggest threats to the city — Banten and Mataram.

They decided to talk to the Mataram empire in Central Java first. The sultan who had ordered the two attacks in the late 1620s had passed away and his sons were embroiled in a fight over succession. That made it easier for the VOC. They simply supported the son that gave them control of the area surrounding the city, specifically defined as the mountains to the south and the Citarum River to the east. That was in 1652. Then, a few years later, they signed an agreement with Banten. Records show that on signing the agreement, they threw a large party with plenty of booze, *sirih*, and dancing. The next day, just to make sure the sultan was not going to change his mind, the Dutch sent over a ship with some gifts, including rosewater and paintings.

These agreements were not always taken very seriously. This became apparent when, a couple of decades later in 1678, Bantenese troops marched to the city of Cirebon straight through the hinterland of Batavia, ignoring the agreements that they had signed. Banten was at the time split into two factions: one led by Sultan Ageng Tirtayasa who vehemently opposed the Dutch, and a faction led by the Sultan's son, Pangeran Hadji, who was more open to dealings with the Dutch. In March 1682, a few VOC ships equipped with heavy artillery arrived in Banten to support the crown prince and drive Sultan Ageng and his supporters from town. Banten was now firmly in VOC hands.[9]

For those living outside the city walls, the immediate danger from marauding armies had passed. From 1660 onwards pieces of land were sold to Europeans with prices pegged to how far it was from the walled city. People then flooded the Ommelanden to grow rice, sugarcane, and vegetables. A few years later, Cornelis joined the stampede and, although there are no records, maybe Barbara or Jacob van der Linde did too. Cornelis writes that it was not until peace with Banten that "we could for the first time discover these lands and bring some order to them. Not much headway was made until 1670, but after that year the region took on a different aspect."[10]

To protect the new plantations and houses against the wild animals and lawless mobs that lived in the forests, fortifications were needed. The first one of these forts was Rijswijk, about an hour's walk south of the city wall. Another one, Jacatra, was erected near two large mango trees, which is known in Malay as *mangga dua*, a name that lives on in its namesake district in north Jakarta today. Several other forts were built and eventually the city was surrounded by an outer ring of six forts that

VUE DU FORT NOORTWYCK, GEZIGT van 't FORT NOORTWYCK,
en venant de Jacatra. als men van Jacatra komt.

A drawing of the Noordwijk defense fort with a canal in the foreground, circa 1749–1779.
This is roughly where Jakarta's Istiqlal Mosque is situated today.

spread out, fan-shaped, a few kilometres from Batavia. These were Fort
Ancol and Jacatra in the east, Fort Rijswijk and Noordwijk in the south,
and Fort Anke and Vijfhoek to the west of the city.

****

Europeans often leased the newly acquired plots of land to the Chinese to
run sugar mills. But one group of people quick to move outside the city
walls – partially because many did not have the means to build a brick
house in town – was the Mardijkers.[11] These were slaves from Portuguese
settlements who had been set free, often after they converted to
Christianity. The name Mardijkers has its origins in the Malay word *merdeka*,
meaning "freedom". In those days, Mardijkers were easily identified by
their clothing: traditional striped trousers, Portuguese silk shirts, hats

and, to the amazement of many Europeans, they wore no shoes. They spoke Portuguese, a language commonly used in Batavia and the Ommelanden until the late eighteenth century. They attended the Portuguese Church just outside the city walls, one of Jakarta's oldest surviving buildings that still operates as originally intended. To make money, many Mardijkers worked in the sugar mills further south, or bought land and built one themselves.

Some Mardijkers settled in an area near Batavia called Tugu – taken from the third and fourth syllable of the word "Portuguese".[12] Here, the links to their Portuguese origins were maintained over the centuries though their language, folklore, kinship, cuisine, music, and religion. This

Detail of the Mardijker in the foreground of Beeckman's 1661 painting (see pages 48–49). Mardijkers were freed Portuguese slaves. Many of them were of Indian origin and poor, and went around barefoot. In the painting, Beeckman added shoes.

unique, Portuguese-influenced identity is acknowledged and treasured: Portuguese ambassadors to Indonesia have visited Kampung Tugu, while their Keroncong Tugu musicians have performed at the Portuguese embassy in Jakarta.

Like the Mardijkers, the Chinese was another group that took full advantage of the opportunities the Ommelanden offered. Large groups arrived after China relaxed its prohibition on overseas trade in 1684. Many sailed to Batavia to set up shop, start trading and invest in the sugar mill business in the Ommelanden. But these newer Chinese arrivals had no connection with the existing Chinese families who had since 1619, the very early days of Batavia, lived inside the city. This meant that the tightly knit Chinese community started to unravel, as the Chinese Kapitein within the Batavia city walls had little control over the Chinese who lived and worked outside the city walls on sugar mills. A few decades later, this would prove to have dramatic consequences.

One Chinese entrepreneur who played an important role in the early development of the Ommelanden was Phoa Bing Gam, a Kapitein of the Chinese community who was known simply as Bingham by the Dutch. In the south of the city not far from Fort Rijswijk, he purchased some of the red, fertile land that the Mataram soldiers a decade earlier had referred to as *tanah abang*. There he established several plantations and in 1648 had a canal dug from the city all the way south to his plantations to allow for easy transport of his sugar, vegetables, and fruits to the markets in Batavia. The canal proved to be very useful, so the Batavian government bought it over from Bingham and renamed it Molenvliet (Mill Canal).[13]

This canal would become a prominent feature of the city in the centuries to come. Aside from transporting goods, the canal was used for

View along the Molenvliet canal going south from the "water plaats", a water collection point. The road is now Jl. Hayam Wuruk. The drawing is made opposite the current location of the Pancoran Tea House on Jl. Gajah Mada.

****

public bathing and washing by the people in nearby houses and estates that gradually developed along the canal. The canal is still in use, but bathing and washing would these days be a toxic experience in the polluted waters. Today, it divides two main highways from the city centre to north Jakarta – Jl. Hayam Wuruk and Jl. Gajah Mada.

In the seventeenth century, the Molenvliet canal provided Batavia with a supply of fresh water. A clever set of locks lowered the water level when needed, making it easier for people to collect water. Every day, after a short walk from Batavia through the Nieuwpoort or New Gate (now Jl. Pintu Besar), slaves would arrive at an area of the city called Pancoran, just south of the city where the Molenvliet canal extended further south, to collect water in jars.[14]

The word for this "waterfall" in Malay is *pancoran*. Soon, Pancoran, as the area became known, became popular and coffee shops and teahouses sprang up to supply drinks and snacks to those waiting their turn at the communal water source. The street exists today as Jl. Pancoran, and the prominent Pancoran Tea House still stands. Around 1663, a Chinese Kapitein called Gan Djie and his wife were the owners of that teahouse and every day, presumably as a gesture of good will, they offered eight pots of tea for free to thirsty travellers passing by. Gradually, this became a tradition called Patekoan – *pa* means "eight" and *tekoan* means "tea pots".[15] Today, the current owner of the Pancoran Tea House keeps this tradition alive by preparing eight pots of tea on a daily basis.

Bingham was not the only one digging canals. Others spotted similar opportunities and built canals to connect the city with the forts in the Ommelanden. Two canals (*gracht* in Dutch) – the Bacherusgracht and the Ammaniusgracht – connected the west of the city to Fort Angke and Vijfhoek. One is still visible as one drives along Jl. Pangeran Tubagus Angke in north Jakarta. Another canal went straight from the east of the city to Ancol and the River Sunter.

After these canals were dug, the next step was the construction of roads to connect all the forts and canals. To round this off, a very long road was constructed from the eastern forts of Ancol and Jacatra at the location of the two mango trees – Mangga Dua – all the way down and inland to Meester Cornelis in the far south, the spot where the Bandanese pastor had acquired some land a few decades earlier. This long north-south axis was called the Zuiderweg ("southward way") and is still in use, although these days it has different names for different sections: Jl. Gunung Sahari, Jl. Kramat Raya and Jl. Senen. This thoroughfare ran parallel to a road that followed the Molenvliet south towards Rijswijk and, eventually, an east-west connecting road was constructed to create a large rectangle.

The paving of roads came with some unexpected benefits – the joy of road trips. Batavia was not built for entertainment. Its chief aim was to trade and make money. For a long time, the highlight of the week was the Sunday walk to church to show off a new dress or the latest piece of jewellery. After church, people would meet and drink tea, or maybe pour a stiff Madeira or gin. But they would stay inside the city. Now, with new road access to the Ommelanden, people like Cornelis Chastelein, Cornelia van Beveren and Barbara van der Linde could make weekend trips along the large rectangular road grid. The idea was to rent a horse carriage, leave the city in the morning, head east towards the fort of Jacatra, take a sharp turn south to follow the new road towards Meester Cornelis, turn right towards Weltevreden, Rijswijk and Molenvliet and then, before the sun set and the city gates were closed, return to Batavia. Somewhere around halfway, people would stop for a picnic or a drink.

Meanwhile, while these new canals and roads were changing the face of the city, Cornelis Chastelein was making money and moving up the VOC career ladder. He made so much that he was able to buy the massive Weltevreden estate[16] along the east-west connection between Molenvliet and Senen, where most people would stop on their weekend trip in the

Ommelanden. Weltevreden (later called Gambir, the current site of the city's major railway station) would in later centuries become a pivotal point in the city and is now part of central Jakarta. He had a house on the estate, surrounded by *sawah* ("paddy fields"), sugarcane plantations and a sugar mill. Almost the entire estate is now the Sawah Besar district.

****

Cornelis was not the only one interested in the Ommelanden. Everybody was busy getting their hands on land and moving into the sugar business, with many of the mill workers staying in nearby *kampung*. Sometimes, the VOC also gave away land rights to useful allies. One of them was Aru Patuju, a Sulawesi ally of the VOC who played an important role in allowing the VOC to control the city of Makassar in Sulawesi. The central Jakarta district of Petojo is named after him,[17] and was home to large clusters of Sulawesians who had arrived in Batavia. Immigrants with similar ethnic origins who came to Batavia tended to cluster in small *kampung* around the six small forts, each of them with their own leader. This also made it easy for new arrivals from other parts of the Indonesian archipelago to look up friends and family who already lived in a *kampung* in the Ommelanden, who could perhaps help them find a job or place to stay. Even today we find place names across Jakarta like Kampung Bugis, Kampung Ambon, Kampung Makassar, and Kampung Bali. An added benefit of this for the VOC was the control and contacts on offer by getting to know the heads of each of these *kampung*. But the fact of the matter was that they did not have as much control over people in the Ommelanden as they did in the city of Batavia.

Slowly, Batavia and Ommelanden turned into a multi-ethic cocktail of settlements with Chinese, Javanese, Balinese, Ambonese, Mardijkers, Dutch, Indians as well as the odd German, Dane or Englishman thrown in. This pool of people would come together in a melting pot and children of mixed marriages would in turn marry people from different ethnic groups so that, after several generations, the descendants lost their own ethnic identity. A new identity and community started to emerge with its own, distinctive signature – the people of Batavia or Orang Betawi.[18] Nowadays, these Betawi are seen as the "original Jakartans". In a sense they were the early explorers of the Ommelanden. Meanwhile, the contrast between the Ommelanden and Batavia could not be greater. While *kampung* in the Ommelanden had a distinct Indonesian character, Batavia was a predominantly Chinese city with a seventeenth century-style Dutch castle standing at its centre.

Running a sugar mill required lots of wood. The trick was to keep the fires that boiled the sugary liquid pressed from sugarcane going. Trees were cut down and the Ommelanden was gradually deforested. Plantations also threw trash and waste into rivers and waterways, clogging up the river and the shallow canals of Batavia.

One day, Cornelis was one of the people who called on the recently established district council in charge of matters in the Ommelanden – the Heemraden – to report that a big log was stuck in the Ciliwung River and was clogging up the waterway. It took the Heemraden four days to gather enough people together to try solve the problem, and even then the job was beyond them. Eventually, several days later, the log was cut into smaller pieces, restoring the uninterrupted flow of water into Batavia. But by then the Batavia canals had silted up. In this way, the rapid transformation of the Ommelanden from backwater to business engine would have dramatic environmental consequences several decades later. The seeds of future disaster had already been planted.

In 1691, Cornelis was fired from the VOC for his "weaknesses", presumably a reference to arguments he had with more senior members of the management team. Cornelis had strong views and judged VOC managers to be incompetent and small-minded, running their business "like a small grocery shop" instead of a large trading empire. He also felt the VOC needed to accommodate the local population, instead of just ripping them off. To some of his managers, that was blasphemy.

It turned out that Cornelis Chastelein was a risk-seeker. Finding himself unemployed and heavily invested in land, he decided to purchase even more. This land was located much further south of Batavia's city walls, some 25 kilometres away. A few years later, in 1695, he bought another large parcel of land called Seringsing, now Serengseng Sawah in Lenteng Agung in south Jakarta. This is where in 1997 I first met the family of my future wife, Teni, and where her father told me that he had fought against the Dutch in the war. But in 1704, we find Cornelis in possession of five pieces of land – Depok, Mampang, Cinere and two nameless tracts along the Ciliwung River. He decided to combine them into one large estate and call it Depok, a name that is still used today.[19]

Having acquired all this land, he established paddy fields, sugar plantations, and gardens with the efforts of his slaves. He also constructed a large wooden house where, presumably, he would spend some of his weekends. When Cornelis passed away in 1714, he left all the Depok land to the slaves that lived there. Now free, they formed a commune and made a modest living.

It proved to be a sustainable idea because the commune still exists today. A foundation, the Yayasan Lembaga Cornelis Chastelein, still manages the land and offers education and support to the Depok Christian community. Depok developed into a large town just south of Jakarta proper and is now part of Greater Jakarta. The specific area where Cornelis had his plantation is still called Depok Lama ("old Depok") or Depok Belanda ("Dutch Depok").

The development of the Ommelanden allowed some to amass incredible wealth. All that was needed was some start-up capital, an ability to spot opportunities and some financial acumen. We don't know if my ancestors such as Barbara or Jacob, contemporaries of Cornelis Chastelein, had a similar business sense or were willing to take the same risks. They simply disappeared from the archives.

But this growth in the Ommelanden would have some undesirable consequences and the seeds of disaster were already germinating. Forests had started to disappear. The social fabric of the city started to unravel, creating tensions between those living within the city of Batavia, and those outside. The next generation would have to deal with some of the dramatic and fatal consequences of these big changes. One of them might well have played a pivotal role in the events that took place in the next century.

His name was Johannes van der Linde.

Chapter 4
A Grisly Execution, an Outbreak of Malaria and a Massacre
1700–1750

Batavia's city archives record that Johannes van der Linde entered the world on 5 February 1707. A family coat of arms in a church in the Netherlands is also mentioned, which confirms that he is my great-grandfather many times over, separated from me by about ten generations. What is less clear is how he is related to Barbara van der Linde, the first member of our family to arrive in Batavia back in 1650. As for his immediate family, we learn from the archives that Johannes was (most likely) the son of a Jan van der Linde and his mother might have been Maria Minta. Her surname suggests she may have been a local women or possibly one of Jan's slaves.

The city archives tell us that Jan was sent to jail in 1714 for 22 months for not paying his debts, and that he was buried in the Portuguese church, which still stands in north Jakarta today. But any trace of Jan's grave has long since disappeared. What we do know for sure is that Johannes would spend all his life in Batavia and passed away 35 years later in 1742. During his lifetime, he saw the city grow rich and prosperous before things started to go downhill and eventually descend into its deepest trough.

Johannes was just a little boy when his father was sent to prison and only 14 when his father died in 1721. By then, Batavia and the surrounding Ommelanden were thriving; both were hives of shops, businesses, sugar mills and plantations. Batavia was not only a success, it was now also a beautiful place to live. Francois Valentijn, Dutch explorer, naturalist, preacher and author, was travelling around the Indonesian archipelago at this time and in *Old and New East Indies*, he described Batavia as the "Queen of the East". The Tijgergracht, he wrote, was of such beauty that it was not to be matched by any canal in Holland itself.

We don't know where Johannes lived in the city, but maps and paintings give us a pretty good idea of what it looked like when he was a young man. At the harbour, workmen and slaves loaded and unloaded ships in the heat of the day, carrying bags of spices or boxes of porcelain up and down the quay. Near the warehouses, administrators would stand in the shade of the tamarind trees, spitting *sirih* and recording the movements of these cargo. Some slaves were known to swallow valuable nutmeg pits and later "recycle" them. After a good wash, they could be sold to Chinese spice traders. On the other side of the quay, across the river, Johannes would have seen the imposing Sapphire and Ruby castle battlements. To the distant south, hazy blueish mountains – Gunung Gede and Gunung Salak – were visible.

Walking south along the river he would hear the hammering of the carpenters on the wharf, busy repairing ships, barges and sampans under a high roof that protected them from the sun. Next to the wharf were men repairing sails. Behind it was a building named Vierkant ("The Square"),[1] but better known as a place where sailors gathered to consume local *arak* in large quantities. Johannes would have been familiar with the spectacle of barefoot, half-naked drunks brawling or drawing knifes until either the local guards showed up or one of the men was flattened or stabbed.

Passing the wharf, Johannes would see the riverside bazaar where people gathered twice a week to buy fruit, vegetables, meat, cloth, and homemade *kueh* (cake). Small barges carried people over the river to the east side of the city where Johannes would find himself right in front of the castle where several VOC warehouses were located. An alley lined with four rows of tamarind trees led from the castle straight to a bridge that was raised at seven o'clock each evening. From there, it was a straight walk south along Prinsenstraat (Prince's Street) to the City Hall. Next to this street was Herenstraat (Gentlemen's Street), better known as Theewater Straat (Teawater Street) given the multitude of Chinese teahouses, where for a little money one could drink as much tea as one desired.

Johannes would pass the east-west Leeuwinnengracht that crossed the famous north-south Tijgergracht which ran parallel to Prinsenstraat. Small boats would navigate these canals to carry fruit, fish, meat, slaves, and other merchandise around town. There were also barges that collected drinking water at Pancoran and circumnavigated the city canals with water sellers shouting "Water!", "Agua!", "Air!" in Dutch, Portuguese and Malay. If somebody wanted water, for a small fee they would carry two buckets over their shoulders into the kitchen. The Tijgergracht was lined with large brick houses where small stairs with iron rails allowed visitors to step up to the entrance. The outside walls were covered with porcelain tiles leading the eye higher up to small protruding roofs depicting images of angels, clouds and birds. The roof allowed the owner to smoke a pipe outside his house without getting wet when it rained.

Heading further south along Prinsenstraat, crossing the bridge over the Leeuwinnengracht, Johannes would end up at the square in front of the City Hall. This is where over a century ago, Coen had Sara whipped in front of the open windows. It would be in one of the dark, stuffy cellars under the City Hall where his father Jan was locked up for 22 months. Maybe his mother would, once every few days, send him over to slip past the guards to pass rice or some fruit to his father. On the west side of the square was the recently finished, octagon-shaped New Dutch Church with a dome that was high enough to function as a beacon for ships at sea. Because of this, the church was also known as Gereja Kubah ("dome church"). It was designed by the local baker, which might explain why it was severely damaged in an earthquake in 1739. The church stood where today the Wayang museum is located. In front of the New Dutch Church guards ensured that only those who were properly dressed entered the building.

Continuing Johannes' journey south, he would go along New Gate Street that ran between the City Hall and a string of shops and restaurants that extended south from the New Dutch Church. During the lunch break, carpenters and craftsmen came here to buy rice with vegetables and a small piece of meat wrapped in banana leaves. He would pass the hospital on his right, and cross a bridge to end up at the New Gate that marked the southern border of the city. Further east was Jassen Bridge that led to the Portuguese Church outside the city wall. If Johannes left the city over the New Gate Bridge, he would have to make way for merchants and plantation owners on horses entering the city to do business.

Outside New Gate, Johannes would enter Outer New Gate Street lined with Chinese shophouses from where, further in the distance, he would be able to spot the crowds waiting to collect water at Pancoran. This is also where some Europeans rented horses and carriages for those who wanted to visit the Ommelanden for a weekend activity or inspect a sugar mill. Walking along the street, he might hear the energetic drums of a group of Chinese musicians at a wedding.

Leaving Pancoran behind, he would now enter the Ommelanden. A wide dirt clay road lined with tamarind trees followed the Molenvliet canal further south. This is where the crowded city made way for the vastness of paddy fields and sugar plantations, at irregular intervals interrupted by large country houses erected by the wealthy eager to escape the crowded city. After walking for half an hour or so, he would approach a junction at the end of the Molenvliet canal, near Fort Rijswijk. The junction acted as a funnel, redirecting traders who arrived from different directions towards the Tanah Abang market, or *pasar*. This is where the Mataram army had set up camp nearly a century ago, naming the place after its red earth.

In the opposite direction of Tanah Abang a road led east beyond the Weltevreden estate towards the Monday market, or Pasar Senen. At the time, many of these *pasar* were established near or on the estates of high-ranked officials, gradually becoming central focus points in the Ommelanden. Gradually, as the population of the Ommelanden swelled, these *pasar* moved further inland so that in 1751, Governor-General Jacob Mossel allowed himself a *pasar* on his estate in Lebak Bulus.

Many of these markets sold all kinds of produce, including fruit, bamboo, and textiles. Some specialised, like the buffalo market established in Meester Cornelis. Pasar Minggu in south Jakarta is still known, even today, for fruit traditionally sold by farmers and traders who arrived from the lush mountain slopes on Sundays to sell their produce (*minggu* is "Sunday" in Malay). Over time, these *pasar* became the focal points of a network of markets in the Ommelanden where people settled, traded and lived. Some eventually emerged as city districts. Tangerang, Bekasi, Senen, Pasar Minggu and Tanah Abang were initially all markets but they now make up whole districts within Greater Jakarta.

****

While the growth in the Ommelanden offered plenty of business opportunities, it also bred feelings of insecurity among some of the Dutch who were surrounded by a growing group of indigenous Indonesians and Chinese. The Dutch were very much in the minority; on the streets of Batavia Chinese was the most common language spoken followed by Javanese, while Mardijkers conversed in Portuguese. While Johannes van der Linde might have felt comfortable within the city since he was born and bred there, this was not the case for all Europeans. They were well aware of the threat that the indigenous Indonesian population represented, which is why only the Chinese were allowed to live within the city walls of Batavia. The Javanese and other Indonesians had to find a place outside.

Indeed, the Chinese enjoyed a privileged position in the city. Some Dutch inhabitants who had previously worked for the VOC but were now running their own businesses – the free burghers – felt that the Batavian government often favoured the Chinese over them. While the VOC was eager to keep its monopoly and restrict free burghers from trading across the archipelago and other parts of Asia, Chinese junks sailed from Batavia to China and Japan to trade their goods freely. This unease amongst some of the Dutch created an environment ripe with suspicion, gossip, and false accusations. And so, in August 1721, when fireworks burned down a large part of a wharf during a Chinese festival, some believed it was not an accident.

This feeling of insecurity reached new heights a few months later, with fatal consequences for a man named Pieter Erberveld.[2] His German father had arrived in Batavia back in 1668, and had been sure to have his wife and children baptised. Baptism and marriage transformed his wife, a former slave from Siam (Thailand), into the lady Elisabeth Erberveld. Their half-German, half-Siamese children – Sara, Johannes and Pieter – were registered as Europeans but were never fully accepted in Batavia society, which was based on rank in the VOC and birth in Holland. At some point in 1721, Erberveld lost his job at the VOC, which might well be why he held a grudge against the Dutch. There was little evidence of mutual love anyway: in a Dutch commentary of the time, Erberveld is described as "big and tall, his eyes showing trickiness and arrogant behaviour".

According to the city archives, he planned to take his revenge by overthrowing the city's VOC leadership and putting himself in charge.

The following is a description of the gruesome events that unfolded after the conspiracy came to a head on the evening of 28 December 1721, although the archives only tell one side of the story and should be taken with a grain of salt.

A Javanese nobleman, Raden Karta Dria, and his entourage made his way through Batavia, crossing the Jassen Bridge and passing the Portuguese church just outside the city walls. From there he turned right towards the Jacatra fort and made his way to the house of Pieter Erberveld, somewhere midway between the fort and the Portuguese church. He knocked on the door, three times hard and three times soft, upon which it opened and he was guided inside by a slave woman who showed Raden Karta Dria the way to the garden at the back of the house where Erberveld was waiting for him.

That evening, these two men discussed their plan to attack Batavia on New Year's Day. Their aim was to kill all Christians in the city and replace the Dutch government with Pieter Erberveld as the new governor. In their efforts to overthrow the government they were to be supported by troops delivered by Batavia's antagonists, the cities of Banten and Cirebon. After a short discussion to iron out some of the final details, the archives tell us that some of the men went to conduct their *maghrib* prayers, suggesting it was around six o' clock in the evening.

Unbeknownst to them, two other events took place that evening, with fatal consequences. First, one of the slaves in the house heard the discussion in the garden. Alarmed by their plans to kill all Christians, he made his way to the house of the city prosecutor, a certain Mr Kroese, to inform him of the plot. Kroese then walked over to the residence of Governor-General Hendrick Zwaardekroon who, at around ten o'clock in the evening, was just about to finish his dinner.

Second, the governor-general had just received a letter from the sultan of Banten informing him of Erberveld's plan to overthrow the government.

Presumably, the sultan had judged that there was great advantage to be had in providing this information to Zwaardekroon, or maybe he thought it better to deal with the devil he knew rather than this unknown Pieter Erberveld. Whatever his reasons, he sealed Erberveld's fate. The letter included the names of all people involved in the plot.

Later the same evening, Erberveld and Karta Dria found themselves surrounded by Dutch soldiers; others whose names the sultan had so conveniently provided were also arrested. Under torture, some confessed to the plan to take the city and pointed to Erberveld and Karta Dria as the main architects.

To make sure everybody understood the consequences of rebelling against the Dutch, the two men were put to death in the most brutal way. A scribe at the time captured their public execution in hideous detail:

> They were tied to a cross backwards, their right hand was cut off, glowing rods were used to burn the skin on arms, legs and the breast and meat taken from it; then, from below, the body was cut open, the heart to be taken out and thrown in their faces, the head was cut off and the body was cut into pieces and heads put on poles and left for the birds.[3]

The execution took place in front of the square just south of the castle, near the gallows, so people could gather and witness the spectacle. Johannes van der Linde was a teenager at the time and he may well have been among them as the execution would doubtless have been the talk of the town.

But that was not the end of it. To make sure these events would not be easily erased from history, a stone pillar was erected in Erberveld's garden. On top of it was a skull pierced by a spear. Underneath, written in both Dutch and Javanese, was a stark reminder:

A Grisly Execution, an Outbreak of Malaria and a Massacre

As a detestable memory of the punished traitor Pieter Erberveld, nobody shall now or ever be allowed to build, to carpenter, to lay bricks, or to plant in this place. Batavia 14 April 1722.[4]

This stone pillar stood in its original location until the Japanese demolished it in early 1942. It was later moved to the garden behind the Batavia City Hall, now the Jakarta History Museum, while a replica is on show in the Taman Prasasti Museum in central Jakarta. Strangely, the date on the stone is about a week earlier than when the actual events took place. This is possibly because the stone was erected much later and the dates got mixed up. Supposedly – there is no proof – the grave of Pieter's accomplice Raden Karta Dria is situated near a mosque on current day Jl. Pangerang Jayakarta.

The monument raised in remembrance of the Pieter Erberveld affair. The text, in both Dutch and Javanese, states that it is forbidden to build or construct anything on this location. A skull sits at the top of the monument.

The whole Erberveld affair was highly suspicious. His trial was not conducted in the normal way, and aside from the testimony of the people arrested, there was little proof of a widespread conspiracy. The whole case was based on inconsistent confessions obtained under torture. To complicate matters further, at the time, Governor-General Zwaardekroon, who presided over the whole affair, was busy acquiring land around where Erberveld lived. Still, in an environment of rising anxiety about large groups of indigenous Indonesians living outside the city walls, the allegations must have looked genuine to many of the Dutch residents. The city recovered quickly from this dramatic episode but racial tensions would come back to haunt Batavia a few decades later.

****

Meanwhile, Johannes van der Linde had found a job with the VOC and was making his way up the career ladder. The archives tell us that he was working as an administrator in 1733 when a mysterious disease hit the city. Thousands died after a short but intense fever, often accompanied by hallucinations. It was described by one Dutch source as "a very miserable and sad disease or paralysis that creates great confusion in the brain".[5]

The number of victims rose alarmingly. The disease made no distinction between poor or rich – Governor-General Dirk van Cloon was one of the unfortunate souls who lost his life. But Europeans were more vulnerable than the Chinese population. For a long time, it was believed that it was heavy consumption of tea that made the difference. But Europeans who tried to protect themselves by drinking copious amount of Chinese tea were not spared either.

The economic effects were devastating. Many sailors died from the disease, so boats with precious cargo could not depart for Amsterdam as there were not sufficient men to make up a crew. Sending new men from

Holland did not help either as about half of all new arrivals died within six months of getting to Batavia. The situation was desperate, and in 1734 a general day of prayer and fasting was declared as the people turned to God and asked him "to lift this plague from the city".[6]

Johannes van der Linde was one of the lucky ones to escape the infection, and we see in the archives that his career was starting to take off. In the mid-1730s we find him running a small shop within the walls of the castle that especially catered for VOC employees. In 1737 he was promoted to chief administrator at the warehouses on the west side of the city and by March 1740 he was installed as the deputy Chief Purchase Officer at the castle. A few months later, he was promoted to Chief Purchaser and only a month later he also took on the job of Captain of Administrators, a title that later would be found on a church memorial plate in his hometown in the Netherlands. While he may well have been a very able and competent man, the death of many senior VOC employees from fever might also have been a factor in his swift ascent up the ranks.

Much later, doctors convincingly argued that the disease was malaria. The coastal area just north of the city had silted up and small ponds of brackish water were left behind during low tide, turning the whole area into an ideal breeding place for mosquitos. The problem was made worse by saltwater fishponds dug by Javanese fishermen in 1729 and which took several years to construct. From the silted brackish waters to the fish ponds, it was a just short flight for mosquitos to reach the walled city.[7]

What did not help either was a proliferation of new and illegal dams and sluices built to direct water to the new estates in the Ommelanden. Decades earlier, Cornelis Chastelein had already complained about logs in the river preventing water from flowing to these estates and the city of Batavia. The current in the Ciliwung River was often weak as the river had started to dry up. This allowed seawater to seep into the canals, inviting mosquitos to breed in the canals inside the walled city.

Something needed to be done. In 1732, Governor-General Diderik Durven ordered the construction of another canal — the Mokervaart — to solve the water supply problem in the Ommelanden. The idea was to connect the Krukut and Grogol rivers to provide a water supply to estates located between Fort Vijfhoek and Fort Rijswijk. Initially, this looked like a good plan but it turned sour when the new canal failed to create better water circulation in the Batavia canals and carried mud into the city instead, speeding up the whole silting process.

Batavia, once referred to as the Queen of the East, gradually turned into an isolated, malaria-infested dump. The British jokingly noted that the mere thought of Batavia's filth and unhealthiness would keep other nations from attempting an attack on the city. The problem did not go away. More than 100 years after the first wave of malaria hit Batavia, an Englishman called John Crawfurd observed:

The Dutch, unmindful of the difference of some 45 degree of latitude, are determined on having a town modelled after those in The Netherlands, within six degrees of the equator and the level of the sea. The river, spread over the town in many handsome canals, lost its current, deposited its copious sediment, and generated pestilent malaria.[8]

The increase in the size of Batavia and its population, combined with the rampant growth of sugar mills and plantations in the Ommelanden, meant the city had reached an ecological breaking point. As a result, those who had the means started to build houses outside the city walls. They would travel to Batavia during the day for work and then retreat to their estate in the evenings. Batavia had its very first commuters.

Johannes van der Linde may have been one of them. We know that by now he had attained a senior position which would have allowed him to build a house outside the city, away from the disease-ridden, stinking canals. We do know that he needed more room – he married twice, the last time in 1740 to Anna Christina van Tile, who was at the time 17 years old.

****

The future of Batavia now clearly lay beyond the city walls and this allows us to tell the story of the Weltevreden estate. From humble origins, it eventually covered most of the southern part of the current Sawah Besar district in central Jakarta, from Jl. Pos near Hotel Borobudur to Jl. Prapatan just south of the Gatot Soebroto Army Hospital. But in the early seventeenth century, Weltevreden was just an open field.

In 1648, a man called Anthonij Paviljoen was granted ownership of a piece of land south of the city near the Noordwijk fort that he used to graze buffalos. Over the years it has carried a variety of names, from Paviljoen Field to Waterlooplein and the name that is in use today – Lapangan Banteng, or Buffalo Field.[9]

Cornelis Chastelein, one of Batavia's great success stories whom we met earlier, had acquired the land and developed what was to become a huge estate. Life must have been good as he named it Weltevreden, which means "well content". The estate was laid out on the east-west axis between Molenvliet and Senen, near where many would stop for a break on their trips outside the walled city.

After Chastelein died, the estate switched ownership several times until 1733 when it came into the hands of a man called Justinus Vinck. This was just when the malaria outbreak was thinning the population. Vinck allowed the estate to act as a connection between Pasar Senen to the east and Pasar Tanah Abang to the west. The roads that connected these markets and the Weltevreden estate are still there – Jl. Prapatan and Jl. Kebon Sirih – and in effect, became one of the city's first east-west connections. Over time, a multitude of governor-generals owned the Weltevreden estate, which at one time contained the city's most spectacular mansion. Unfortunately, no trace of it remains today and the area is now the centre of government and littered with a number of different ministries.

While Batavia was meticulously planned, the Ommelanden was characterised by the absence of a master plan. The area's development was a process of organic, incremental growth where geographical features, such as hills and bends in rivers, combined with a road network around the markets, determined the shape of this new part of the city.

Key engines of growth in the Ommelanden were the sugar mills, mostly run by Chinese and some Mardijkers. While the Chinese in the city were under the close supervision of the Chinese Kapitein, this was much less the case in the Ommelanden. Many were new arrivals from China with little or no connection to the Chinese in Batavia. The Chinese Kapitein, such a dominant figure in the Chinese community in Batavia, often found himself bypassed by these new arrivals. For example, they did not pay taxes to him.

This was a challenge for Ni Hoe Kong, the Chinese Kapitein in the 1740s and a contemporary of Johannes van der Linde.[10] The Kapitein was wealthy and ran a textile trading business with his four brothers. He also owned a considerable amount of land, had 14 sugar mills in the Ommelanden and lived in a large house in Batavia on the west side of the river, a few blocks from the wharf on Roa Malaka. We also know from the archives that he made considerable financial contributions to the churches in Batavia.

Life was generally good for Ni Hoe Kong, but problems started to emerge with the collapse of the sugar market. Back in the 1720s, demand for sugar in the Middle East had dried up and sugar prices fell dramatically. Within a few years, many sugar mills were forced out of business and bands of jobless outlaws were soon roaming the Ommelanden. Robbery became more common and slowly the Ommelanden turned into a local version of the Wild West.

What did not help was a series of increasingly arbitrary measures adopted by the VOC in Batavia. By 1739, the Chinese city population was larger than the Mardijkers, Europeans and mestizos (people of mixed race) combined; in the Ommelanden, they were the largest group after the Javanese. To control the size of the Chinese population the VOC issued residence permits. Those who did not have permits were picked up and in some cases, shipped off to Ceylon (Sri Lanka).

In early 1740, rumours made their way around town that a group of Chinese on their way to Ceylon were thrown overboard midway by the Dutch. True or not, for a group of frustrated, jobless Chinese in the Ommelanden, this was enough to declare war. They wanted to drive the Dutch from Batavia and take control of the city. In preparation, they gathered around sugar mills in Tanah Abang.

In late September 1740, Governor-General Adriaan Valckenier received a message that bands of Chinese in the Ommelanden were rioting. He and the ruling Indies Council initially ignored the warning, feeling safe within the city walls. They were more focused on infighting and power politics within the council itself, especially between Valckenier and his chief antagonist Gustaaf van Imhoff, a senior VOC official who was previously the colonial governor of Ceylon. He was also the man who build Toko Merah ("red shop" in Indonesian), a building that, because of its colour, stands out in old Batavia and over time was a residence for a string of governors, a shop, a hotel and an office building.[11]

But by 4 October, the Council started to get worried as reports of groups of frustrated Chinese roaming the Ommelanden continued to come in. They decided to send reinforcements to strategic locations and some fifty solders were sent to Meester Cornelis. Additional soldiers were also deployed to support fortifications in Tanah Abang, Angke and

Noordwijk. It soon became an armed conflict. The first Dutch attempt to disperse these bands of Chinese failed as the attack was disorganised and the men lacked supplies. But the next day, Friday, 8 October 1740, the Dutch tried again with some success.

We know that Ni Hoe Kong made a trip that day to Tanah Abang to try to talk with the barricaded Chinese, but with little success. By noon, he had returned Batavia to report back to the governor and his council. Later that day, bands of Chinese surrounded the city and set fire to the southern suburbs. A Dutchman wrote in his diary that it was an ominous sight, with fire and smoke visible and the sounds of Chinese war cries and the beating of drums from beyond the city walls. Johannes van der Linde was there and must have feared for his life.

The next day dawned on a city gripped by fear. Chinese shop owners kept their shops closed and the streets were deserted. Women and children stayed at home while some had been able to escape the city during the night by boat to the sea. Rumours sweeping the city suggested that some Chinese were supporting their countrymen outside the city walls. Others suggested that Ni Hoe Kong must be heavily involved with these attacks.

That morning Ni Hoe Kong made his way from his home in Roa Melaka on the west side of Batavia to the castle. It is uncertain what was discussed and if he met with Governor-General Valckenier. But we know from the diary of a certain George Schwartz[12] that a Dutch sailor attacked a Chinese man near the warehouses on the west side of Batavia, not far from Ni Hoe Kong's house. Dutch and Chinese men hurried to the scene to join in the fight and by eight o'clock in the morning, the brawls turned into random attacks on Chinese within the city. It rapidly developed into a massacre. Europeans started to randomly kill Chinese, plundering and setting fire to houses. Ni Hoe Kong himself narrowly escaped a volley of bullets fired at him by Dutch soldiers while on his way back home from the castle.

Historian Ary Huysen provided this eyewitness account:

Suddenly we heard to our great consternation nothing but cries
of murder and fire, and the curtains were raised for the most
abominable scene of unrestrained murder and rapine: Chinese
men, women and children were run through with the sword.
Neither pregnant women nor babies in arms were saved. Captives
in irons, altogether a hundred people, had their throats cut like
sheep. Dutch burghers who had provided shelter to many well-to-
do Chinese fellow citizens killed them on the same day so that they
could partake of their victim's possessions. In short, the Chinese
nation was almost totally massacred that day, guilty or innocent,
all and sundry.[13]

People who under normal circumstances would loathe violence, now
engaged in orgies of murder and plunder.[14] German carpenter Georg
Berhardt Schwarz later wrote in his diary that he killed his Chinese
neighbour just because he wanted to steal the man's fat pig. Others
killed Chinese they owed money to. Fights even broke out between the
plunderers while the massacre was unfolding on the streets around them.

Also there was Johannes van der Linde, although we have no record
on what role he played. But as a senior administrator, he was most likely
working in the castle that morning, or was near the warehouses where the
first fights started. In short, Johannes would have been right in the thick of it.

The government did little to intervene. Ni Hoe Kong, dressed as
a woman, tried to escape the city but he was recognised, arrested and
accused of treason, the same charge that sealed the fate of the unfortunate
Pieter Erberveld a few decades earlier. He too was tortured, but he swore
that he knew nothing about the revolt; no evidence so far has come to light
to suggest that he was involved. The council spared his life but banned him

Detail of a print showing the slaughter of the Chinese in October 1740. Cannons are visible on the bottom right.

from the city and he spent his last days in Ambon in eastern Indonesia, never to return to Batavia.

It took three days for a measure of calm to return to the city, although there were still bands of Chinese roaming the Ommelanden. After the massacre, it was ruled that the Chinese had to move outside the city walls. A new *kampung* for them was established just south of the city wall and a number of houses that had been destroyed were cleared to create a large square in front of this new settlement. Glodok Square is still the location of Jakarta's Chinatown.

Johannes van der Linde, who survived the outbreak of malaria as well as the massacre he had witnessed, and possibly even participated in, ran out of luck. Less than two years later, on 15 October 1742, he passed away at the age of 35. The cause of death is not known, but growing old in Batavia was a luxury for the very few. There is no trace of his grave. His family in the Netherlands hung a plaque in his memory in the largest church in Zwolle, near his ancestral hometown. It is still there today.

But Batavia's Chinese population was badly depleted – about 10,000 Chinese had been killed – and many Europeans left the scarred city. The Queen of the East was gone.

Chapter 5

The Travails of Slave Girls and Chinatown Reborn

1750–1800

The lookout shielded his eyes as he scanned the horizon. The rocking of the ship, combined with the waves glittering in the bright sun, made it difficult to see exactly what lay ahead. But slowly, in between the palm trees on the distant coast, the dome of a church came into view. He instructed the cabin boy to inform the officer on watch that they had arrived in Batavia. Captain James Cook sailed into the bay of Jakarta in October 1770 aboard the HMS *Endeavour*. It was the Englishman's first epic voyage for his expedition to the south Pacific Ocean, during which he charted the coastlines of Hawaii, New Zealand and eastern Australia. The crew was exhausted and the ship badly in need of repair, having narrowly avoided shipwreck on the Great Barrier Reef. It was good to be on dry land again.

At the time, new arrivals to Batavia were still ferried from their ships by small boats to what was called the *kleine boom* ("small custom house") for registration and luggage clearance. The Dutch word *boom* literally means "tree" or "barrier" and refers to a wooden beam that was placed over the entrance to prevent smuggling and collect tolls. A little further south was a larger custom house, appropriately named the *groote boom* ("large barrier"). It was used to clear cargo and pay duties and, presumably, this is where Cook and his men stepped ashore.

During his visit, Cook did not seem to have ventured far from the city; if he did, what he saw must not have been of sufficient interest to write about in his journal. But his sailors and captains would often leave the city to hang out at bars and restaurants near the forts in the Ommelanden to play billiards or an early form of golf. They also took the opportunity to feast on fresh meat and indulge in *gloria*, a popular tipple at the time which consisted of *arak* or brandy cooked with sugar, cinnamon and nutmeg.

Ready for an extended break, they stayed in Batavia for nearly three months to repair leaks and stock up on food. Entries in Cook's journal show that he was dismayed it took weeks before he obtained access to Onrust, a small island just north of Jakarta where ships were repaired. It seems a fair number of Cook's men fell ill during their time in the city, and at least seven were lost. A few months later, the day after Christmas, the *Endeavour* felt the west wind on its bare mast and rolled slightly east by five degrees. Sails clattering and the wind wailing through the rigging, it entered the Java Sea, leaving Batavia behind. Later that day, Cook sat down in his cabin to write down his impressions of the city. He was not a fan:

> Be this as it will, Batavia is certainly a place that Europeans need
> not covet to go to; but if necessity obliges them, they will do
> well to make their stay as short as possible, otherwise they will
> soon feel the effects of the unwholesome air of Batavia, which,
> I firmly believe, is the Death of more Europeans than any other
> place upon the Globe of the same extent. Such, at least, is my
> opinion of it, which is founded on facts. We came in here with
> as healthy a Ship's Company as need go to Sea, and after a stay
> of not quite 3 months left it in the condition of an Hospital Ship,
> besides the loss of 7 men; and yet all the Dutch Captains I had an
> opportunity to converse with said that we had been very lucky,
> and wondered that we had not lost half our people in that time.[1]

The Travails of Slave Girls and Chinatown Reborn

****

Unlike Captain Cook, most people who took the trouble to explore the Ommelanden had a much more favourable view of the city. Take the Dutch naval officer and explorer Stavinorus, a contemporary of Cook.[2] In his notes he described trips he made through the Ommelanden which provide us with a picture of what it looked like around 1770.

From the city, he wrote, there were five main roads that spread out like a large fan (see map on page 54). The first road meandered to Ancol in the east, where Bujangga Manik, the wandering hermit-monk from Pakuan, visited some two centuries earlier. Stavinorus noted that the road followed a small river, adjacent to wide gardens and fields criss-crossed by beautiful small creeks. Upon arrival in Ancol, he saw a large estate, not far from the beach, where Europeans went at the weekend to escape the city, relax and indulge in local delicacies such as oysters.

The second road was to the southeast towards Mangga Dua and – as its name suggests – lined by two rows of mango trees. There were some gardens here but Stavinorus considered these to be not as beautiful as those near the third road a little further south, the Jacatra road (now Jl. Pangerang Jakarta). It was there that Stavinorus was seriously impressed by "extremely beautiful" gardens, streets lined with tamarind trees and small fruit plantations. "I have never seen a more beautiful road ever," he wrote, and "everyone that is a new arrival in Batavia is surprised from such a beautiful sight and that in a land, of which people in Europe have low expectations."[3] He also observed that this third road continued south to Weltevreden along Gunung Sari.

The fourth road went straight south from Batavia and followed the Molenvliet towards Tanah Abang, where Stavorinus mentioned a Saturday market where people from further afield came to sell vegetables and fruits. This was the same road that Johannes van der Linde had walked down so

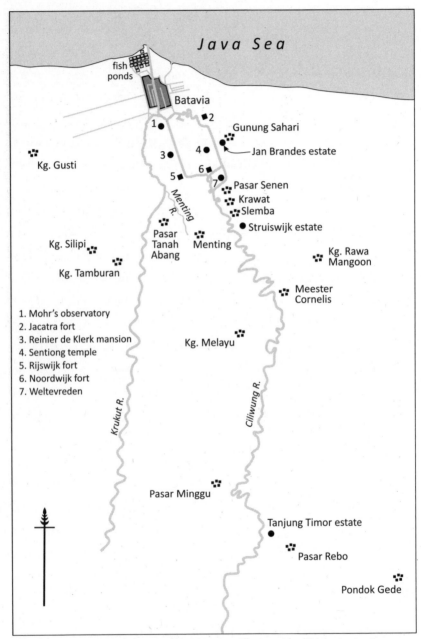

Batavia and the Ommelanden with the location of key *pasar* (markets), *kampung* (settlements) and estates. These were the central nodes around which the city would grow over time.

often a few decades earlier. Lastly, the fifth road pointed westwards in the direction of Angke, and also followed a river. He ended his commentary by observing that all those roads were made of hard clay and that they were accompanied by paths for pedestrians.

These five roads became the five axes along which the city slowly crawled inland. Like ivy following the branches of a tree, the city grew along the roads that led to markets that sprung up in the Ommelanden, gradually moving south.

****

We have snapshots of what life was like at the end of the eighteenth century for certain groups of people thanks to the paintings of Jan Brandes, an artistic Lutheran minister.[4] He sailed to Batavia in 1776 and lived there for six years. Soon after arrival his wife gave birth to a son, also named Jan, but she died a few months later. The widower raised his son with the help of four male and four female slaves, whom he often depicted in his artwork. A prolific painter, Brandes had an eye for detail and a great interest in flora, fauna, and his surroundings.

Theevisite in een Europees huis in Batavia ("Tea Visit in a European House in Batavia") depicts two Batavian ladies having tea in a reception room with large sash windows, while two slaves in *sarong* attend to them. One of the ladies is clearly of mixed origin and she is enthusiastically engaging with the European lady, who is listening attentively and sipping her tea. The marble table, paintings on the walls and Chinese porcelain at bottom right reinforce the sense of lavish decoration. Outside stand two more slaves, one of them cooking over a small fire.

Huis en landgoed Brandes buiten Batavia ("The house and estate of Jan Brandes on Batavia") shows that he lived in the Ommelanden, and illustrates the scale of his house in relation to his estate.

Jan Brandes' depiction of a mestizo woman (seated, left), receiving a European guest (seated, right) for tea. On the left, a slave holds a box of *sirih* (betel nuts).

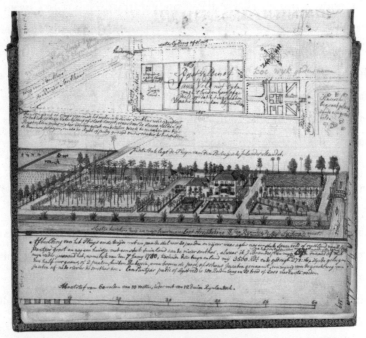

A watercolour by Jan Brandes of the white one-storey house, outbuildings, stables and estate outside Batavia where he lived from 1780 to 1785.

The Travails of Slave Girls and Chinatown Reborn

****

A view of Batavia city in the 1770s. This drawing shows City Hall, the square in front of it, the octogonal Dutch church on the right and the Tijgergracht on the left.

The expansion of houses and shops along the roads from the city to the Ommelanden accelerated after the 1740 massacre when the Chinese were ordered to move outside the city walls. Most moved to Glodok, the new Chinatown south of the city wall, near the road along the Molenvliet.

To ensure the Dutch could keep an eye on the Chinese population in Glodok, land was cleared for a square that later became known as Glodok Square. This area remains Chinatown in modern Jakarta, although the square is now gone. Molenvliet is also still there, the canal now sandwiched between two large thoroughfares (Jl. Hayam Wuruk and Jl. Gajah Mada) which carry traffic from central Jakarta to old Batavia in the north.

Many Chinese built their new shophouses in the labyrinth of streets behind Glodok Square, especially favouring a bend in the river now called Jl. Blandongan. This is also where Masjid Al-Anshor, thought to be Jakarta's oldest mosque, is located, in an area where many Bengali and Gujurati traders used to live. The mosque is still in use today. Along these streets we also find one of Jakarta's oldest Chinese temples – the Jin De Yuan temple or Wihara Dharma Bhakti – which became a central focal point in this new Chinese district. Nor far away is the Candra Naya building on Jl. Gajah Mada, where an old Chinese mansion has survived the centuries, now surrounded by shopping malls.

With Kapitein Ni Hoe Kong banished to Ambon after the 1740 massacre, fresh Chinese leadership was required. A new Chinese Council, the Kong Kuan, was installed and one of its first moves was to restore the Jin De Yuan temple which was partially burned down in the massacre. But the council did more than restore buildings. It also acted as a judiciary. The Kong Kuan would meet every Wednesday at a residence in Batavia to listen to plaintiffs and claimants and settle problems such as unpaid debts, stolen goods, marriage problems, extortionate interest rates on loans and, if need be, even send people back to China to settle debts.

One of the cases was heard on 14 November 1787, when a certain Wu Yuan-guan came before the Kong Kuan.[5] He said that he had purchased a female slave in Bali and arranged for her to accompany him to Batavia as a passenger on the ship of a captain called Zhong Lai. He had wanted to sell her in the Batavia slave market but after sailing for a few days she became hysterical. The captain, also in attendance at the council, said that she "screamed and wailed for most of the night" to such annoyance that he thought she had gone mad.

Wu argued that the captain had ordered him to throw her into the sea. But that meant Wu would have no means of repaying his debts; he had come to the council to have the captain pay the price of the slave.[6] With clinical detachment and little regard to the fate of the Balinese woman, the Kong Kuan proceded to gather more information and ordered witnesses to come forward. One went on record stating that "the female slave whom

Wu Yuan-guan bought was already demented and had lost her mind in Bali" and that upon learning she would be of no value at all in Batavia, it was Wu Yuan-guan himself who had thrown the lady into the sea. While this appeared to put the captain in the clear, the council could not come to a final agreement and referred the case to the Dutch authorities. The final verdict is lost to history.

****

While the Kong Kuan helped rebuild a new Chinatown, more Europeans were eager to escape the city's stinking canals and diseases. To them, Batavia became a place to do business while they lived in houses or mansions just south of the city, along the five streets detailed and admired by Stravinorus. One of these mansions is still there today, just south of the Chinese Glodok square along the Molenvliet canal, and is currently used by the Museum of National Archives. It belonged to Reinier de Klerk,[7] an ambitious sailor who climbed the career ladder to become a member of the colonial government, the Council of Indies. He was appointed Governor-General in 1777. At first sight, the residence looks like a Dutch mansion transported to Java, but closer inspection shows its builders had mingled Dutch and local building practices to develop what was later called the "Indisch" style.[8] The massive estate contained a mansion, stables and separate housing for slaves, all surrounding a large garden.

One of the guards at the estate was a Polish Jew with the cumbersome name of Jehoeve Leip Benjegiehiel Snijder, later changed to Leendert Miero.[9] He was a contemporary of Captain Cook and Stravinorus. One day Miero made the mistake of being found asleep when Reinier de Klerk returned home. For this, he received fifty lashes and was dismissed. He swore revenge.

Looking for a new occupation, he became a goldsmith in nearby Glodok. Business must have been brisk as Miero made money and acquired a house and land some 25 kilometres south of Batavia. Just like some of the other estates in the Ommelanden, Miero's became the focal point for a Wednesday market – Pasar Rebo[10] – while the estate itself was nicknamed Pondok Gede ("large hut"). Both are still names of districts in south Jakarta.

Miero continued to prosper and by 1819, over 40 years after being fired, he was in a position to acquire Reinier de Klerk mansion. By that time, his former master was long dead and the property was in the hands of de Klerk's widow. Miero enjoyed his revenge – he acquired the estate and started a tradition of throwing a large party on the anniversary of the day he received the whipping. After he passed away, the mansion switched owners several times and was eventually acquired by the Dutch government to house an archive. Later, the Indonesian government made it a museum.

The Reinier de Klerk mansion, circa 1930. Today, the building houses the Museum of National Archives.

****

Events in Europe also made an impact on the city. Wars had weakened the Dutch economy and it became increasingly obvious that powerful players such as France and England were now calling the shots in Europe. The port cities of London and Hamburg were overshadowing Amsterdam as centres of international trade. London was establishing itself as a key financial centre, also at the expense of Amsterdam. In 1795, Napoleon Bonaparte annexed the Netherlands and continued to wage war across the continent until he was defeated by the Duke of Wellington at the Battle of Waterloo in 1815.

In the meantime, the French were in control of the Dutch colonies, including Batavia. As a result, the city became more isolated from the motherland and ships from Europe arrived far less frequently. Although never fully cut off, it found itself increasingly detached from the Netherlands. While citizens wrestled with the new order, often dividing loyalties, one thing was clear – Batavia was going to have to rely much more on itself.

One consequence of these conflicts in Europe was that after 1780 the trickle of white women sailing to the Indies virtually dried up. Dutch men from higher ranks found it increasingly difficult to find suitable European wives.[11] They often turned to local women, whom they took on as wives, slaves, concubines or temporary sexual partners. Regulations regarding children born outside marriage were loosened, so sons and daughters from these relationships were now considered legitimate. Outside Batavia, in cities dotted along the north Java coast, it was not unusual to find Dutch men with harems.

The daughters of wealthy European officials of high office were in great demand. These young women became pawns as families vied with each other to establish the strongest business and social relationships. Sons, on the other hand, had to make their own way in the Indies and with education in Batavia pretty limited, their career paths were often long, arduous and uncertain. Indeed, after 1727 the government announced that "Indies children" – that is, Europeans born and educated in the Indies – would only very selectively be employed in government services. Higher ranks were only for those educated in Europe, so the preferred route was to send boys home to the Netherlands to be educated. This was expensive and the option was only available to the wealthy upper echelons of Batavian society. Back in the Netherlands, these young men would stay with family or a foster parent and many would sail back to Batavia after they had finished their studies.

To find a job, they would often use their father's network of friends and colleagues. A much sought-after role was that of Commissioner of Native Affairs, which gave the official control over the lands surrounding Batavia. These commissioners ruled like kings. Selling licenses and dealing with land issues allowed them to rake in a fortune. Another very lucrative position was administrator of the island of Onrust, where ships were repaired – including Captain Cook's – and where the VOC warehouses were located. Men stationed on the island supplemented their incomes with bribes and contraband.

But while sons were sent away to be educated, daughters stayed in Batavia and married. In effect, they formed the social glue for the upper classes. For men, their position in society was measured in terms of their rank at the VOC.

This was taken to extremes by General-Governor Jacob Mossel. Already known for his prolific issuance of new laws, he secured himself a place in history with the so-called Mossel's code. It codified etiquette in minute detail and included "Measures for Curbing Splendour and Magnificence". There were regulations about the number of horses allowed to pull a carriage, based on VOC rank. The code also stipulated that the use of a glass carriage was reserved for the governor-general himself. There were laws that stated that only persons higher than the VOC rank of under-merchant could carry an umbrella or *payung*, although European women were allowed to use them too. And only men with the rank of upper-merchant were allowed to wear clothes with buttons. Velvet clothing was only appropriate for women married to men of the highest VOC ranks. In effect, Mossel's code was a sumptuary code that tied the display of wealth and status to rank within the VOC hierarchy.

But this picture of Europeans as lord and master while natives laboured in the paddy field or kitchen is incomplete and simplistic. Local women as well as children of mixed marriages (known as mestizos), could become part of this elite, often through baptism and marriage. This was how Pieter Erberveld's family established themselves in Batavia in the late seventeenth century. There were also numerous uneducated Dutchmen struggling to make a living and had low-ranking jobs within the VOC. At the same time, there were those with a penchant for gambling, womanising and drinking. Unfortunately, it is in this category that some of my ancestors seemed to fit best.

One of these Dutch souls in Batavia was another Jacob van der Linde, who emerges from the archives in 1793. We don't know if he is a direct relative of Johannes van der Linde, the senior merchant who was in Batavia during the massacre in 1740. Neither do we know when Jacob was born. We also find records of a Helena Maria van der Linde, who married in 1752. She could have been his sister, with her second name Maria referring to her mother, Maria Minta.

Initially, Jacob's medical career started off well and he was promoted to chief surgeon at a hospital in Batavia. But he seems to have inherited a lack of financial acumen from his ancestor, Jan van der Linde, who was sent to jail in 1714 for 22 months for unpaid debts. Jacob, too, quickly ran into financial problems despite his well-paid position. We don't know for sure, but perhaps he made some bad investments or frequented gambling dens and taverns a bit too often for his own good.

In 1793 he was allowed to delay the repayments of debts to a man called Gerlach Cornelius Johannes van Nassau in light of Jacob's pending wedding to Anna Catherina Kleyns, presumably a widow with money. These debts seemed to have been settled after his wedding but a few years later, in 1796, Jacob had run up new debts, this time to a Pieter van der Weert. And in the same year, additional debts to another man, Wijbrand de Jong, were recorded.

It seems that these debts were also settled, presumably again with the help of his wealthy wife Anna. She was probably not pleased but for the moment the marriage was stable and in May 1799, Anna gave birth to Charles Pieter Gerardus van der Linde. But a few years later, the archives record that Jacob adopted Jacoba Rosetta van der Linde, a girl he fathered with Portia van Siam, presumably a slave. Jacoba Rosetta was baptised on 31 October 1802. Anna was not amused, and the records show that a few months later Anna and Jacob were divorced.

****

Marrying a wealthy widow was also an easy route to fortune for German-Dutch Reformed pastor Johan Maurits Mohr.[12] Born in Germany, he arrived in Batavia in 1737 as a church minister. Mohr was an unusual creature as he was more of a scholar than a trader. Upon arrival, he decided to learn Portuguese, which was still widely spoken in and around Batavia then. Shortly after his wedding in 1752, he started the construction of a mansion near Molenvliet, close to the Reinier de Klerk estate and next to the Jin De Yuan temple that by then had been fully restored by the Kong Kuan.

By that time, Mohr had caught the astronomy bug. He wrote several books and reports, including one about the 1761 transit of the planet

Venus. This was a watershed moment in the history of astronomy as it was the first time the size of the solar system was accurately measured. His books and writings raised his status as a local scholar and in 1765 he received permission to construct a large observatory on top of his house. This was not just an amateur attempt. Mohr purchased quality equipment, had it shipped over to Batavia and built an observatory unsurpassed in Asia for another 150 years. It became a centre of attention for scientists as well as an aid for navigation, given that the structure towered well above all the nearby houses and mansions and could be seen from afar. Someone coming from Molenvliet (Jl. Gajah Mada) would have been able to see it at the very end of what is now Jl. Kemurnian in Glodok.

French explorer Louis-Antoine de Bougainville visited the observatory and was impressed, as were some of the members on Captain Cook's expedition, although it is unclear if Cook himself visited. Unfortunately, in the decades after Mohr's death, the meteorological and astronomical work that had made an impression on so many came to a halt and little was done to maintain the observatory. By the end of the century it was turned into lodgings for VOC clerks and then an army barracks. Much later, it was torn down.

Still, Mohr's observatory created a spark. Bataviaasch Genootschap van Kunsten en Wetenschappen (The Batavian Society of Arts and Sciences) was founded by a group of enthusiasts in and around town. Sadly, Mohr never got to play a major role as he died soon after the society was founded. Most of the members were Dutch, high-ranking members of the VOC who met to discuss the Indonesian world around them and to keep abreast with the latest scientific developments in Europe.

Later, local Javanese men also joined the society and contributed to its activities and writings. Over the years these society members collected all manner of things, including fifth-century stones with sinuous inscriptions, remnants of Hindu and Buddhist statues, and relics from temples found across the Indonesian archipelago. Through the academy's printing press they circulated the results of their research. Later, they pooled their private collections to form Indonesia's first museum, now the National Museum on Jl. Medan Merdeka Barat.

****

As the city sprawled southwards, inland and upwards, the massive Weltevreden estate – which ran along the east-west connection between Molenvliet and Senen and where people would stop for a picnic on their weekend trips to the Ommelanden – became an increasingly important location. This was where roads met, markets were established and the wealthy congregated. What made Weltevreden so convenient was the proximity of two large open spaces. The first was initially called the Parade Square, later renamed Waterlooplein and currently known as Lapangan Banteng. As the name suggests, this square was perfect for parades and the government established a barracks nearby for its troops and an officers' club named Concordia. It also was the place to be seen on Sunday afternoons after church. Near this open area was Fort Noordwijk, which was initially established to guard these fields. Noordwijk does not exist anymore but was located just opposite what is today the entrance to Istiqlal Mosque, the largest mosque in Indonesia.

The second open space, further west of Weltevreden, was much larger. It also carried a variety of names, from Buffalo Field, Champ de Mars and Kings' Square (Koningsplein in Dutch) to its current label, Medan Merdeka.[13] Today, this square is where Jakarta's iconic 132-metre-tall National Monument (known as Monas), which was built in the 1960s, pierces the sky. The original square was of sufficient size to practise firing cannons without fear of destroying buildings that lined the sides. Here, the Dutch built large houses, now much better designed to deal with the tropical conditions, along leafy suburban roads and canals.[14] These "Indisch" style houses also expanded along the east-west canal that ran from Senen and connected with Molenvliet. The land south of this canal was called Rijswijk (now Jl. Veteran), a reference to the old fort that was once located nearby. Facing Rijswijk, north of the canal, was the area called Noordwijk (now Jl. Juanda).

New roads and canals criss-crossed these districts. One large road that ran from Molenvliet all the way to Gunung Sari was named Prinsenlaan, currently Jl. Mangga Dua. Jl. Tangki, near Lokasari and Mangga Dua, refers to a water tank that was once located there, while Jl. Batu Tulis translates as "written stone road", suggesting some early form of signpost. Jl. Pecenongan[15] was often used by runaway slaves to escape from their masters. Today, it is Jakarta's culinary centre.

****

It is along these new streets and alleys in Rijswijk and Noordwijk that the tragedy of Tjindra of Bali unfolded.[16] On 25 April 1775, Batavia city surgeon David Beijlon was asked to come and examine a young lady who had been brought into the hospital. She was bruised all over, her ear was torn, her right cheek partially burned and her eyelid was half torn off. The surgeon learned that she was a runaway slave. He later recorded that she was beaten with a slipper, with firewood, and with a rattan stick by her mistress. It was a brutal beating as it took a week before Tjindra was well enough to present herself in front of the court. It is through the diligent work of court clerks that we gain insight into the life of a slave in Batavia.

Tjindra was the property of a woman called Oetan. Her husband, Amat, had purchased Tjindra as a wedding gift for his wife. At the time, many slaves came from Bali and were put to work at home or on plantations.

Tjindra's situation was slightly different as she had to find work during the day and then pass on any money she earned to Oetan. We don't know what kind of work she did but many slaves would do laundry at the Molenvliet, squatting beside the canal and rubbing clothes over stones.

It seems that Oetan was not happy about the amount of money Tjindra was bringing home every day. She accused Tjindra of putting some aside for herself. This resulted in regular beatings. One evening, Tjindra arrived home smelly, sweaty and covered in dirt from her day's work. An angry Oetan thrashed her with a rattan stick and ordered her to wash herself. When Tjindra took too much time to clean up, Oetan flew into a rage and beat her again with the rattan stick, a slipper, and a piece of firewood.

That night, Tjindra waited until everyone was asleep and quietly slipped out of the estate into the dark streets of Batavia. Perhaps she tried to get to Jl. Pecenongan, which led into the woods and fields surrounding the city. This is where many slaves could melt into the local *kampung*, although police guards under the leadership of a *landdrost* (steward) often worked with community leaders to track down these runaway slaves. But she did not make it that far. In the early morning servants on a nearby estate found an exhausted Tjindra and carried her to the hospital where David Beijlon saw her.

The subsequent court proceedings were most unusual for that time. Legal cases involving the abuse of slaves in Batavia rarely reached the courts. The general view was that slaves needed discipline, so physical punishment was routine. As the case began, Oetan and Tjindra were both subject to questioning by lead prosecutor Jan Hendrik Poock. The slave's testimony obviously carried considerable weight as Oetan was ordered to pay all the legal costs related to the case. But it is a stretch to say justice was served. Although Tjindra was permitted to leave what was clearly a very violent household, she was simply resold on the slave market with the proceeds going to the court. There is no trace of what became of her.

****

Meanwhile, by the close of the eighteenth century, most people were making their living outside the city. The city had become run-down and desolate. Schools that taught Dutch closed for lack of pupils, and church-led charity for the poor dwindled as finances dried up. Isolated and malaria-infested, the city had a petty, parochial feel about it. It seemed that Captain Cook had been right about the place.

Mohr's observatory had fallen into a state of decay, but his work had at least kindled interest in science, Indonesian culture, flora, and fauna. This was unusual in a town where making money was the chief objective. Meanwhile, the wayward and debt-prone Jacob van der Linde passed away in 1809, some six years after his divorce from Anna. Leendert Miero, the self-made man who owned a grand estate and celebrated his own whipping every year, continued to grow his fortune until his death in 1834. The struggling city continued to expand, gradually populating the Ommelanden. But in the next century, events in Europe would again dramatically reshape the contours of the city.

Chapter 6
Moving the Capital, British Invasion and the First Taste of Luxury
1800–1850

Jan Pondard[1] took the pipe from his pocket, knocked the bowl against the palm of his hand and stuffed it with tobacco. He then walked over to his neighbour's shop and took a small stick from the fire and lit his pipe. He was ready to start the day.

Jan owned a small shop in Outer New Poort Street, right outside the old city gate on the street heading towards the Pancoran, across from the famous Pancoran Tea House. It was here that he offered his expertise in the repair of marine timekeepers. In the early 1800s, seafarers measured their latitude by the sun's angle at noon – the further south, the lower the sun. But to determine longitude a timekeeper was required, as being further west translated into a larger time difference with the port of departure. To ensure the clocks ran with mathematical precision, captains would often make their way to Jan's shop straight after paying cargo duties at the *groote boom*.

Jan also repaired fashionable small pocket chronometers and he noticed a growing demand for freestanding, weight-driven pendulum clocks, some of them damaged on the journey to Batavia. Still, his real affection was for large, brass-bound, mahogany-boxed marine chronometers. He had wanted his shop to be located near the harbour, but his wife had vetoed the idea, telling him that old Batavia had the stench of dead fish and was the cause of all kinds of diseases. Outer New Poort Street was a compromise: it was outside the old city gate but only a short walk to the harbour.

His shop was a maze of boxes filled with thousands of tiny toothed wheels, brass hour indicators, springs, escape wheels, pallets and less easily identifiable components that drove the mechanism of a clock. In the back was a large table where he dissected timekeepers with surgical precision. It was a sweaty, hot, suffocating place. Jan had ignored his wife's suggestion to install small windows to let the light in, afraid that a gust of wind would blow his systematic assembly of minuscule watch components into disarray. "Rather take a bath every day," was his reply. At least it gave him an excuse to cool down outside on the street in the shade, pipe in hand.

Jan was in Batavia at an interesting time. He would get to witness the dramatic transformation of the city in the first two decades of the nineteenth century. Other witnesses were Charles van der Linde, the child of Anna and Jacob, and Jacoba Rosetta van der Linde, the illegitimate daughter of Jacob. During their lifetimes, a new town emerged further south on the Weltevreden estate. The old part of the Batavia became the commercial hub where the shipping and trading companies had their offices and warehouses. Weltevreden was home to the government, military, and a wide variety of shops. The two were connected by the Molenvliet canal and a road that ran alongside it.

****

To understand what happened in Batavia, we also need to look at events in far-away Europe. In 1795, Napoleon Bonaparte had annexed the Netherlands and appointed a new governor, Herman Willem Daendels, a Dutchman who had fought for the French in Europe. He arrived in

Batavia in 1808, promptly fixed civil servants' salaries and prohibited these officials from getting involved in trading. This was not good news for Jan Pondard's business as a decent chunk of it came from wealthy civil servants, who now had less money to burn. Daendels also kicked out a number of officials and within a few weeks of his arrival he had achieved the questionable status of being loathed equally by both the Dutch and the Indonesians, who nicknamed him "iron marshal" or *mareskalek guntur* ("thundering marshal").

Meanwhile, with the French in control of the Dutch colonies, their British adversaries renewed their interest in controlling Java. To confront this military threat, Daendels raised an army of 20,000 men,[2] opened an officer's training school in Batavia, and set up arms factories and hospitals. He ordered the troops to practise marching and artillery fire on the open field next to Weltevreden, called the Koningsplein and better known these days as Medan Merdeka.

Having an army was one thing, marching it around Java was a whole other affair. At the time, Java was connected by stretches of small, dirt clay roads that somewhat randomly spread from Batavia and the Ommelanden. During his time as governor of the Dutch East Indies, from 1808 to 1811, Daendels decided to connect existing roads, flatten and broaden them, and build bridges to create the very first highway along the northern coast of Java. This road started on the western tip of Java in the small town of Anyer and finished in Panarukan in eastern Java. It stretched over 1,000 kilometres.

This was the first time that Batavia was properly connected to other cities in Java and over time it was known as the Groote Postweg, or the Great Post Road.[3] It was a major engineering achievement. Roads were dug through mountains, swamps and paddy fields, and bridges were constructed over valleys and gorges, although its construction came at a terrible cost to the many Javanese who were forced to work on it.

Moving the Capital, British Invasion and the First Taste of Luxury

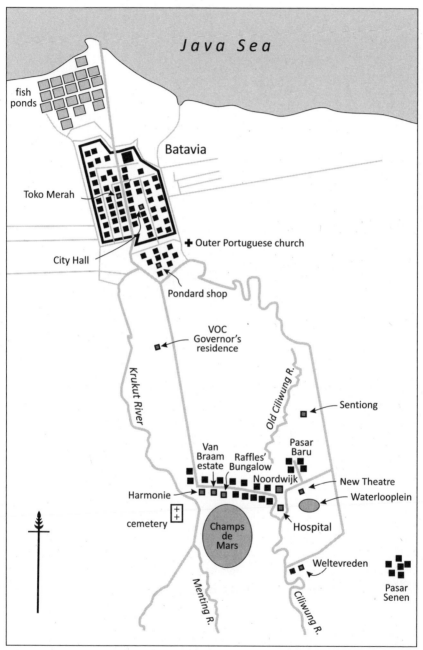

Batavia in the north and the new capital, Weltevreden, established further south, circa 1810. Champs de Mars is today Medan Merdeka (Independence Square), where the National Monument (or Monas) is. The Van Braam estate is now the presidential palace.

****

While European geopolitics were influencing Batavia, the other issue confronting Daendels was the reality that, like Jan's wife, few wanted to inhabit the foul-smelling cesspit that was Batavia. Eventually, around 1810, the call was made: instead of fixing the problems, it was better to move the capital to Weltevreden a few kilometres south, on the elevated grounds of the old Chastelein estate.[4]

This project came with a lot of bells and whistles. First, Daendels ordered the erection of a large French-style palace next to Weltevreden's Waterlooplein, the former Parade Square. Bricks were in short supply, so the old Batavia fort was torn down to provide much-needed building materials. The old castle was left empty, dilapidated and overgrown with weeds. Later, the orphanage on the west of Batavia was also torn down, its bricks finding their way into new shops, houses and a new theatre in Weltevreden. Daendels also closed some of the stinking canals and removed some of the old city gates. Bit by bit, the seventeenth-century fortress of Batavia reappeared as a local adaption of the fashionable French "Indies Empire"[5] architecture style of the day.

The construction of Daendel's palace took longer than expected and when it was eventually finished in 1828, the idea that the governor would live there was abandoned as better alternatives had become available. Instead, it was used as a post office and later to house part of the Supreme Court. Over time, it was nicknamed the "White House" and its current-day moniker is "the Miramis building". It stands at the end of Lapangan Banteng – the current name for the erstwhile Waterlooplein – and houses the Ministry of Finance.[6]

A new church was also required. The Dutch were mostly Protestants but they found themselves under Roman Catholic rule after the French had taken over and the Vatican was quick to jump at the opportunity to

The Roman Catholic Jakarta Cathedral, built in the neo-gothic style. It still stands today and is located next to the Istiqlal Mosque, the largest mosque in Indonesia. This picture was published between 1906 and 1930, and gaslights can be seen in the foreground.

appoint an apostolic prefect in 1807. Initially, mass was held at the home of a Dr Assmuss in Senen, but by 1829 a church had been constructed on the opposite side of the Waterlooplein. It collapsed in 1890 and the imposing Jakarta Cathedral, which still stands today, was erected in its place.

In order to complete all this construction Daendels needed manpower, which was supplied by the *kampung* surrounding Weltevreden. One of these *kampung* was called Gambir; after 1921 it would lend its name to a night market, the Gambir Market. Another *kampung* was Pejambon, an abbreviation of *penjaga Ambon* or Ambonese guards, who looked after a bridge that crossed the Ciliwung River and gave access to the nearby Immanuel Church.[7]

Daendels also needed money. With demand for land in Weltevreden growing, he sold tracts to people who could then build their own mansions in the fashionable "Indies Empire" style, with large rectangular windows, verandas that opened up to wide gardens and high ceilings to deal with the tropical heat. The highest-priced lots were around the Koningsplein. The most lavish of these properties was erected by a wealthy VOC official called Van Braam. This magnificent structure later became the official residence of the president of Indonesia, the Istana Negara. It still stands, facing the large Medan Merdeka square (known as the Champs de Mars, or Koningsplein in Van Braam's days).[8]

Another increasingly popular location was Rijswijk (now Jl. Veteran and Jl. Juanda) at the northern edge of the Koningsplein. Fort Rijswijk was long gone, torn down in 1729, but the name had stuck. Opposite Rijswijk, on the northern side of the canal, was Noordwijk. This is where smaller houses at more reasonable prices were on offer. Civil servants, notaries and other professionals lived in between bakeries, furniture retailers, boarding houses, and restaurants. A little further north along Molenvliet was the growing urban enclave of Petojo, named after the Bugis man from Sulawesi who fought with the Dutch and was given the plot of land in 1663.

****

By early 1811, there were rumours that a British force of 10,000 soldiers had departed India for Java to kick the French out. Daendels was prepared. With a determination that matched his nickname, he wrote to Napoleon that he would rather lose his life than see the British take Java. But Napoleon had different plans. Unbeknownst to Daendels, just as he dispatched that message, a French ship arrived on 15 May 1811 with his appointed successor, Jan Willem Janssens, on board. Daendels was ordered back to Europe. There, he would witness Napoleon's dramatic defeat in Russia.

This change in governor benefitted the British. Governor Janssens had little time to settle in before British landings east of Batavia were reported in August 1811.[9] These troops made their way to old Batavia, which they took with little effort as it was defended by a single officer and 43 Javanese soldiers. The Dutch army retreated further south of Weltevreden to the old

Struiswijk estate (now Salemba) and Meester Cornelis (now Jatinegara). That is where they decided to dig in and await the assault.

Horologer Jan Pondard had a ringside seat. On the morning of 10 August, British commander-in-charge Colonel Hugh Gillespie gave the sign to his troops to march slowly from Batavia, past Jan's shop and the Molenvliet canal, towards Weltevreden. Most shops in the street had closed that day and the streets were empty but Jan stood outside his store, pipe in hand, and watched the British troops march past.

The untrained, disorganised Dutch forces were no match for the British. The invasion force first overran the few troops remaining in Weltevreden and then set their sights on Meester Cornelis, where the rest of the Dutch forces were stationed. They took their time to reorganise and then attacked on 26 August. Once the bullets started flying, chaos ensued in the Dutch ranks. There was one chance to retake the initiative when a few men, in charge of defending a redoubt, surprised the British forces. When it was clear the redoubt could not be defended, they decided to blow it up. The enormous explosion confused the advancing British forces. The Dutch and French forces ran off to Buitenzorg (Bogor) from where they fled into Java's interior via the newly built Groote Postweg.[10]

Initially, the British ended their pursuit at Tandjong-Oost, about ten kilometres south of Meester Cornelis. In the weeks thereafter they were eventually able to capture Governor Janssens. Now a prisoner of war, he was put on board a ship for London that departed Batavia on 18 October 1811, five months after his arrival. The British were now in control of the Indies and Batavia reported to Calcutta, the headquarters of the British East India Company. The new governor was Sir Thomas Stamford Raffles who installed himself, along with his wife Olivia, in a bungalow next to the Van Braam residence in Weltevreden. Raffles went on to make a major contribution to the expansion of the British Empire, and was probably best known for the founding of Singapore in 1819.[11]

****

With the war over, life for people like Jan Pondard returned to its normal, gentle pace. But by 1813, business was slow as fewer and fewer ships arrived in Batavia. This meant that nautical chronometers were not going to be enough to sustain business. The future was in selling and repairing watches, chronometers and pendulum clocks to a new urban elite in Weltevreden. To get their attention, Jan decided to advertise, both in English and Dutch. One morning in July 1813, Jan stepped out of his shop and made his way to the Pancoran Tea House to buy a copy of the *Java Government Gazette*. He returned to his shop, made space on his table littered with wheels and opened the newspaper. At the bottom of the front page was what he was looking for:

Advertisement.

THE Subscriber, J. PONDARD, having been shipwrecked on the coast of Java on his passage to the Mauritius, by which misfortune he has lost the little earnings which several years labour and industry had gained him, being returned again to Batavia, begs leave to inform his friends and the public, that he means to establish himself in the Watch and Clock-making line at Ryswyk; and hopes by an unremitting attention and close application to his business, united to the desire of giving satisfaction, to merit encouragement and support from the public at large. —Persons living on remote parts of the Island may depend on his paying due attention to any commission they may favor him with in the line of his profession.

J. PONDARD.

BATAVIA,
July 22d 1813.

The Subscriber, J. Pondard, having been shipwrecked on the coast of Java on his passage to the Mauritius, by which misfortune he has lost the little earnings which several years labour and industry had gained him, being returned again to Batavia, begs leave to inform his friends and the public, that he means to establish himself in the Watch and Clockmaking line at Ryswyk, and hopes by an unremitting attention and close application to his business, united to the desire of giving satisfaction, to merit encouragement and support from the public at large. Persons living on remote parts of the Island may depend on his paying due attention to any commission they may favor him with in the line of his profession. J. PONDARD. Batavia, July 22nd 1813.[12]

To reach clients across Java, he advertised in the widely circulated *Java Government Gazette* instead of newspapers that focused more on Batavia. It was his wife who had suggested the text and come up with the idea of spicing up the story by mentioning his departure to Mauritius a few years earlier that had ended in a dramatic shipwreck.

****

The British interregnum proved to be a short one. Following Napoleon's defeat at the Battle of Waterloo in 1815, peace was brokered in Europe. The Dutch would get most of their colonies back, including the Indies. Stamford Raffles and his administration packed up, departed and a new Dutch governor was sent in. The Indies were back under Dutch control again, but this time, it was not the VOC that was running the show. The former trading giant, riddled with corruption and burdened by bad business decisions, had been limping along for several decades and was finally declared bankrupt in 1822.

What was left of the VOC offices, warehouses, and trading posts were merged into a new company, the Nederlandse Handel-Maatschappij or NHM (Netherlands Trading Society).[13] Its scaled-down operations were, from February 1826, managed from an office in old Batavia, on the east side of the Ciliwung River and a short walk from Jan Pondard's shop. It was known as the Factorij, a word harking back to the glory days of the VOC. Unfortunately, white ants took a particular liking to its inventory of spices, coffee, and tobacco, and operations were forced to move to another building on the opposite side of the river, between what are now Jl. Teh and Jl. Kunir.[14] Much later, in the 1930s, it would move again to a building opposite the Kota train station that currently houses the Museum Bank Mandiri. The word "Factorij" is still prominent on the front of the building. The design was the work of three architects; one of them, a certain C. van der Linde, was probably also one of my ancestors.[15]

The resettlement from Batavia to Weltevreden coincided with an increase in the size of the non-Dutch population. The British had closed the Batavia slave market, which meant that new arrivals from Bali, Makassar, and elsewhere were now absorbed into the local kampung. Later, Dutch control over Java led to a surge in the number of Javanese and Sundanese looking for jobs in Weltevreden. Meanwhile, the slow demise of the VOC diminished the supply of European emigrants to Batavia just when, as if to compensate for this, an increasing number of Chinese, Indians, and Arabs arrived on its shores. The make-up of the city's residents was changing rapidly.

The new Weltevreden residents needed easy access to daily household goods, food and clothing, so bakers, butchers and other retailers were setting up shop in Weltevreden. There were also markets selling provisions and daily necessities in Glodok, Tanah Abang and Senen. These were all easily accessible, but far from the new residential centres of Noordwijk and Rijswijk. A new market was required. Daendels' government had already acquired land just north from Weltevreden and given it the rather unimaginative name of Pasar Baru, or "New Market". In 1821, it was a wet market and in 1825, space was rented out so people could set up shops.

Chinese traders were eager to move into Pasar Baru and they were soon followed by Arabs, Indians, Malays and a few Europeans. Initially, conditions in this market must have been both cramped and dangerous. In 1859, a fire burned down 94 bamboo houses and a year later, another fire destroyed part of the market. Over time, Indian traders came to dominate; even today it is called Jakarta's "Little India".

By the 1820s, the intermixing of people and cultures was so extensive and differences between distinct ethnic groups were blurred to such an extent, that Indonesians born in Batavia and Weltevreden began to be called Orang Betawi ("Batavia people"). Most were Muslims, had their own customs and wedding ceremonies, their own style of houses and

Giant, festive puppets called *ondel-ondel* at a celebration in modern-day Jakarta.

a distinctive Malay dialect. One tradition was the appearance of *ondel-ondel* – giant, colourful puppets that swayed on the move and livened up celebrations, weddings and, if needed, chased evil spirits away. The Orang Betawi lived in the *kampung* surrounding Weltevreden and had their own security guards who, in case of fire or other emergencies, would hammer on drums hung on trees.

While Weltevreden was a new urban centre, these *kampung* were semi-rural. There were frequent newspaper reports of locals falling out of coconut trees, tigers lurking in forests or people being devoured by crocodiles. Hunting parties often went out to catch game in the immediate surroundings of the city.

****

After the British left, the Dutch wanted full control over Java. This was achieved after they quashed a local rebellion in Central Java led by Prince Diponegoro, who was captured, interned in the prison in Batavia, and later banished to Sulawesi. Soon after, the Dutch introduced new agricultural policies that made farmers poorer and Dutch traders and their native allies enormously wealthy. These traders were the nouveau riche who threw money around Weltevreden, bought property and demanded new luxuries.

The *Bataviasche Courant* of 4 December 1819 shows retailer Rijk, Prediger & Co. advertising a recently received shipment of "red medoc, port, white Bordeaux, champagne, German wines and heavy Amsterdam beer".[16] Also available were other luxuries such as anchovies, herring, Dutch chocolate, cashmere, flannel, lace socks for women, French and English porcelain, mirrors and guns for hunting. The VOC might have been gone, but for some a new party had started.

These traders also demanded the latest French fashions and a prominent new arrival in town was renowned men's tailor Oger, who opened a store strategically located between Rijswijk and Noordwijk at the very end of the Molenvliet. On the first day of December 1841 he announced in an advertisement:

> P. Oger, clothes maker from Paris, announces to the public that
> he has associated himself with the gentleman J. Kuiff, and they
> have erected a well-stocked shop in Noordwijk in the house that
> previously belonged to gentlemen Groen, where available are
> sheets, satin lines trousers, silk vests, sewed shirts, ties, suspenders
> all after the latest fashion and at very agreeable prices.[17]

Two decades earlier, Jan Pondard had made the same move when he closed his shop near the Pancoran Tea House and followed his new customers south (that land was a little higher, so people referred to it as going "upwards") to Noordwijk, although it seems he still had some business from ship captains to repair nautical equipment. We find his advertisement in the *Javaansche Courant* on 2 December 1820:

> Pondard, Watchmaker, has removed to Noordwyk, and informs
> the Commanders of vessels, that he receives Chronometers
> for repair, and to regulate them the necessary instruments for
> observation being with him. In case of difficulty to send them
> up to Noordwyk, Mr. Schaider, Outer New Poort Street, will
> receive and forward them.[18]

This advertisement is the last trace of Jan Pondard. Six years after the opening his new shop, Mrs Pondard boarded a ship heading for France, never to return. The ship's record shows that she travelled alone.[19]

Several of my ancestors were contemporaries of Jan Pondard. After the British had chased out the Dutch forces in 1811 and put Stamford

Raffles in control, a young lady by the name of Albertina Catherine van der Linde married Englishman Robert Lucy in 1812. Elsewhere, there are reports that a Willem van der Linde was buried in Noordwijk in 1808 and his son Hermanus van der Linde was, together with a Marie Sophie Kouwenhoven, declared dead by a doctor in January 1832, although the cause of death is unknown. In 1829 there are newspaper reports of troop sergeant A. van der Linde being injured in a battle during the Java war. The following year he gets a promotion to first lieutenant but after that he disappears from the archives.

We also pick up the trail of Jacoba Rosetta van der Linde, the daughter of Jacob the surgeon who fathered a child with his slave Portia van Siam. This was presumably the source of much discontent in Jacob's household and the reason his wife Anna divorced him soon after. Jacob died a few years later in 1809 and his daughter Jacoba ended up in the Batavia orphanage on the west side of old Batavia.

Jacoba's life was short and grim. She was cut off from any family inheritance, had no father and never married. Her mother's name suggests she came from Siam (Thailand), so Jacoba probably had no extended local family in the *kampung* she could fall back on. Living conditions in the Batavia orphanage were miserable,[20] with women and girls sleeping on wooden floors, huddled together like animals in what some described as a "pig's cot".[21] Bathing facilities were filthy and an unpleasant stench from the canal that bordered the orphanage penetrated the rooms. During the day she would try to make some money, probably by sewing. Some young female orphans were lucky and met young men willing to marry them. Jacoba was not one of them and she died at the age of 21. The orphanage placed an advertisement in the *Bataviasche Courant*[22] to inform those who had lent her money to make a claim so they could be paid off with what little she had left behind.

Her half-brother, Charles van der Linde, the son of Jacob and Anna the rich widow, fared much better than his unfortunate half-sibling. It is fair to assume that he lived comfortably somewhere in Weltevreden. He probably inherited his mother's wealth but there is no indication that he was in any way interested in helping Jacoba. His name appears in ship records in the 1830s and we find him travelling between Batavia, Semarang, Surabaya, and Amsterdam. At one point he is registered as carrying pieces of tin, which suggests he was a merchant trading metals. He died in Surabaya in 1869.

****

We get another view of what life was like at the time thanks to an observant Chinese traveller who, notebook in hand, arrived in Batavia in the late 1830s. His name was Ong Tae Hae. He first wandered the streets of old Batavia and wrote that "the streets are lined with shops, and the markets thronged with barbarians, high and low, holding business, so that it may be truly said, profit abounds in those southern seas."[23] Clearly, the commercial heart of old Batavia still had a strong pulse.

He then made his way to Weltevreden which had by then been transformed into a leafy town of large streets lined with tamarind trees. With the exception of the very poor, few walked the streets. Horse-driven two-seat carriages known as *sado* and two-wheeled wagons called *delmans* – after their inventor Deeleman – rushed through the streets as people made their way to shops and offices.

Home deliveries were common too. Weltevreden residents sat out on verandas waiting for hawkers to sell them fried rice, *sateh*, fried bananas, *bakso* (meatball soup), *jamu* (a health tonic made from turmeric, ginger and other spices) or iced drinks. Street vendors dropped by carrying an array of household goods and toys or offering to repair clothes. In the evenings, candles and lights spread a faint light over the shrubs and trees in the garden and neighbours dropped by for a chat on the veranda, glass of wine in hand.

Ong Tae Hae seemingly enjoyed Weltevreden much more than Batavia, praising the landscape and architecture:

> gardens and parks of the Hollanders adjoining one another,
> for miles together. There you have high galleries and summer
> pavilions, bridges and terraces, so elegant and beautiful as almost
> to exceed the compass of human art; the extreme skill and
> cleverness displayed in erecting them no pen can describe.[24]

He also wrote that food was cheap in Batavia. A pack of rice could be bought for a small amount of cash and ducks and fowls were even cheaper than vegetables. And, "for a mere trifle you can get your own attendant". But, coming from China, some European manners were completely alien to him. He found it odd that men and women mingled together and considered many of the Dutch people he met extravagant and self-indulgent. Elsewhere, he approved of young men who bowed to their elders. But what absolutely baffled him was the strange practice, repeated every Sunday, of closing down one's business to visit a church. He must have peeped inside the house of prayer because he wrote that:

> [E]very seven days there is a ceremony day or sabbath when from
> nine to eleven in the morning, they go to the place of worship, to
> recite prayer and mumble charms; the hearers hanging down their
> heads and weeping, as if there was something very affecting in it
> all; but after half an hours' jabber they are allowed to disperse and
> away they go to feast in their garden houses and spend the whole
> day in delight without attending to any business.[25]

Neither was he impressed by the lack of entertainment and, seemingly, any form of intellectual discourse in the city:

... there are no writings of philosophers and poets, wherewith to beguile the time; nor any friends of like mind, to soothe one's feelings; no deep caverns or lofty towers, to which one could resort for an excursion; all which is very much to be lamented.[26]

Ong Tae Hae failed to mention evening street performances by local artists making money as magicians, balloonists, *wayang* puppet masters or dog-and-monkey showmen. Popular too were groups of young people playing *keroncong* on the street, a mixture of Portuguese and Indonesian music which sounds bit like a distant relative to fado folk music. Perhaps he found this all a bit too lowbrow for his refined tastes.

Societeit Harmonie.

Welteureden.

The Harmonie Club at the very southern end of Molenvliet canal. This square is now called Harmoni but the club is long gone. This picture, taken between 1895 and 1908, also shows the French fashion retailer, Oger, on the left.

Neither does Ong Tae Hae mention the Harmonie, a club that catered to the higher echelons of society in Weltevreden. It was located just behind the Van Braam residence, at the end of Molenvliet, opposite the Oger menswear shop from Paris. This is where successful businessmen such as Charles van der Linde would go for dinner, have a drink, play cards, smoke a hookah or cigar, or read a newspaper in the large, high-ceilinged reading rooms. Once a month the Harmonie hosted a ball, an opportunity for the wealthy and well connected to show off, mingle and network. It is also where the governor would celebrate the birthday of the Dutch king. The Harmonie building is long gone, but the whole area located at the very end of the Molenvliet canal still carries its name.

****

European entertainers travelled to Weltevreden, now hosting a new *schouwburg* ("theatre") built using bricks from the old orphanage in Batavia (currently the Jakarta Art Building, or Gedung Kesenian).[27] It proved to be a very popular venue and traffic jams of horse-drawn carriages along Rijswijk and Noordwijk became such a nuisance that parking restrictions had to be introduced. Newspapers were full of advertisements for shows there, such as the Friday evening performance of *Les Premieres Amours*, a play in one act, in October 1835 by a French entertainment troupe.

The beauty of Weltevreden did not go unnoticed and the erstwhile title, "Queen of the East", was dusted off to attract visitors to the city. Hotels popped up and the residence that formerly housed Sir Stamford Raffles was turned into the upmarket Hotel der Nederlanden. But the place to be seen in was a new colonial hotel named Hotel des Indes, opposite the Harmonie. It offered spacious luxury accommodation and an even more impressive culinary experience. Of particular note was the popular *rijsttafel*, an elaborate feast with up to 24 small separate portions

Picture postcard of the famous Hotel des Indes along the Molenvliet canal, published circa 1936. On the left is the car entrance with a large, shady banyan tree.

of fried rice, *gado-gado, rendang, gulai, sambal* and whatever else the chef had decided to cook. To digest it all, the rest of the day was filled with slumber and lethargy.

In the 1820s people still liked to make the circular trip from Batavia south to Weltevreden, along Gunung Sahari and return along the Molenvliet, just like Cornelis Chastelein and Barbara van der Linde and so many others had done over a century earlier. But now people ventured further, toward the cooler mountains surrounding Bogor. This city was still a long ride south of Batavia and Weltevreden and the area in between was dotted with *kampung*, paddy fields, dense forest and the occasional house. It was a real adventure to travel to Bogor and there are reports of people having to switch from horse to buffalo wagons to get through the rutted, muddy roads.

A popular place to rest or visit on the Weltevreden-Bogor road was the Tandjong Tjie Jantong estate, a piece of land previously owned by Ni Hoe Kong, the unfortunate Chinese Kapitein who was tortured during the 1740 massacre.[28] It was here that the British forces halted their pursuit after their successful attack on Meester Cornelis in 1811. A Wednesday market was held near the estate, which is why the district is still called Pasar Rebo ("Wednesday market"). Markets were initially known for what day were held on, and these original names according to days of the week remained in use, even as later on, they stayed open all week long. This is the case even today. Remnants of the estate can be found on what is now the corner of Jl. Raya Condet and Jl. TB Simatupang in south Jakarta.

A little further south from the Tandjong estate was the old Chastelein domain in Depok, where descendants of Chastelein's freed slaves continued to farm. They resurface in the archives[29] in 1844 when a family by the name of Gronovius claimed to be the lawful owners of the land and showed proof of direct lineage to Cornelis Chastelein. The family asked for the slaves to leave, the land to be returned to them, and to be compensated. The dispute turned into a string of court cases. Eventually, the Supreme Court ruled that Chastelein's original will had to be respected and the descendants of Chastelein's slaves were indeed the rightful owners of the Depok estate.

By the 1850s, the move from Batavia to a flourishing Weltevreden was complete. The thundering Daendels was by now a faint memory, and Jan Pondard's watch shop long gone. In the next 50 years, the city would continue to expand, which meant that new areas for urban settlement were required. And a painter, Raden Saleh, would put his stamp on the city.

Chapter 7
A Dutch Bestseller, Batavia's Robin Hood and a New School
1850–1900

In 1856, a young colonial civil servant, Eduard Douwes Dekker,[1] resigned from his post as assistant commissioner of Lebak, an area in West Java. He had held a number of government posts but his attempts to protect the Javanese from exploitation by both their colonial overlords and their own chiefs had received little official support from his fellow administrators.

This gallant gesture would have gone largely unnoticed had Dekker, under the pen name Multatuli, not ended up in a small hotel room in Belgium where he wrote *Max Havelaar: Or, The Coffee Auctions of the Dutch Trading Company,* a novel that described in fine detail the myriad abuses that he had observed at first hand. His pen name was derived from the Latin phrase *multa tuli*, meaning "I have suffered much".

The book, published in 1860, quickly became a bestseller and went on to become one of the country's most popular literary works, establishing Dekker's reputation as one of Holland's greatest writers. His novel stirred a public debate about how the country was running its most important colonial possession. Parliament even called ministers to account for some of the scandals described. Eventually, *Max Havelaar* became a catalyst for change in the Dutch East Indies and Eduard Douwes Dekker became an inspiration for some of Indonesia's early nationalists at the turn of the century.

He left behind a substantial legacy (as well as some rather large gambling debts). There is a statue of Multatuli on a square next to the Singel Canal in Amsterdam, the annual Multatuli Prize (a Dutch literary award) is named in his honour, and the Multatuli Museum is located in Amsterdam at Korsjespoortsteeg 20, where he was born.

At the time Dekker was becoming a celebrity by highlighting the horrors of colonialism, European nations were continuing their quest to expand their influence across Asia. The British ruled India and were making inroads into China (they had taken over Hong Kong in 1842) and the Dutch were consolidating their power across the Indonesian archipelago. At the same time, Britain and Germany, the continent's two superpowers, had started to drift apart and their close dynastic, cultural and economic ties were unravelling in increasingly antagonistic ways. By 1914 they were at war.

The Netherlands was in a bind.[2] On the one hand, the country relied on British naval power to protect their merchant fleets that sailed between Amsterdam and Batavia. On the other, its businesses were increasingly linked to the industrial boom in Germany. It tried, with some success, to please both nations. At the same time, the Netherlands invested in new infrastructure like railways and ports both at home and in the Indonesian archipelago. Batavia would greatly benefit from these new projects.

Meanwhile, after a long and bloody war in Aceh, north Sumatra, the Dutch had the run of most of the archipelago and the end of the conflict was good news for trade. Merchants and entrepreneurs arrived in Batavia to buy and sell spices and commodities such as timber and metals, set up notary offices or work as accountants. And the first thing they all needed was accomodation.

****

Back in 1628, when the Mataram army arrived from the east to attempt to wipe the young city of Batavia from the face of the earth – an endeavour in which they eventually failed – the soldiers first needed to rest. Many troops camped out in the forests not far from the city walls. While preparing for their attack, they were struck by the reddish colour of the soil – red earth is *tanah abang* in Javanese – and the name stuck. This area, just west of what is now the large Medan Merdeka square, is still known by this name.

In the decades that followed the retreat of the Mataram army, the VOC saw off a variety of other threats with the result that the land surrounding Batavia became a safer place to live. Tanah Abang was now ready for progress. The Molenvliet canal, dug south from the city in 1648, provided better access and forests were cut down to make way for a variety of vegetable and fruit farms to feed the fast-growing city. Their locations can still be traced in the many street names around Tanah Abang – Kebon Kacang, Sirih, Jeruk, Jahe and Melati refer to the peanut, betelnut, oranges, ginger and jasmine planted there centuries ago.

After the massacre of the Chinese in 1740, the Dutch told the survivors to move out of the old city and some settled near Tanah Abang. A few Arab traders were already selling textiles there and, over time, the Tanah Abang market grew. It must have been an attractive place as estates were constructed nearby and used as weekend retreats by Europeans who wanted to get away from the city. Some started to experiment with different crops – growing rice, vegetables, cotton, tea and various spices – while others raised cattle.

In the eighteenth and nineteenth centuries Tanah Abang continued to grow and when the government moved its seat to Weltevreden in the early 1800s, nearby areas such as Noordwijk and Rijswijk were gradually populated. By the late nineteenth century, new land for housing had to be cleared, creating two new settlements – Menteng and Cikini.

Menteng, just south of the Koningsplein and not far from Tanah Abang, was named after a small creek, the Minting, that is visible on some old maps of the Ommelanden.[3] The creek started near the Koningsplein, roughly where Bank Indonesia is now located, and part of it still flows south between Plaza Indonesia and Kebon Kacang. By the 1860s, a growing number of people started to move to Menteng but soon found that running large estates was a very expensive affair. Slavery had been abolished by now so estate owners had to pay salaries to their many employees. Most opted to build houses that were much smaller than the villas surrounding the Koningsplein. Part of the area came to be called Gondangdia, after the *gandaria* or plum mango trees that thrived in the swampy ground.[4]

As Menteng expanded and more people and shops moved out from Batavia, the authorities decided to move the site of the city's original cemetery. It was transferred to an area called Kebon Jahe ("ginger garden") in Tanah Abang, now called Taman Prasasti and the site of a museum. Along with the graves of many leading Dutch residents, there can be found the tomb of Olivia Devenish, an English woman born in India who became the first wife of Stamford Raffles, the man who was the governor of Java during the brief period of British rule and went on to found Singapore. She was ahead of her time, accompanying her husband at official occasions and on visits to native rulers. Another curiosity is a replica of the skull of Pieter Erberveld, the alleged conspirator who came to a violent end in the early 1700s.

****

The other new focal point for the expansion of the city was Cikini, just east of Menteng and Gondangdia. Here, too, smaller houses were preferred to the estate-sized villas surrounding the Koningsplein. This is where a rather odd-looking building was erected – part-German castle, part-cathedral and part-Arab temple. Completely out of kilter with the rest of the Cikini neighbourhood, this small palace had fancy columns on the front porch spreading all the way out to wings, with spacious verandas on all sides. Closer inspection revealed details such as exotic plants climbing up the columns and small gothic spires on top of the main building. It was surrounded by gardens – though in modern times these have since disappeared, replaced by a large car park.

This architectural amalgamation that is currently part of Cikini Hospital was the brainchild of one of Indonesia's most revered painters, Raden Saleh Sjarif Boestaman, better known as Raden Saleh. Born in 1807 into a Javanese royal family of Arab descent, he moved at a young age to Batavia where his drawings attracted the attention of A.J. Payen, a Belgian painter who was touring Java to paint landscapes. Impressed, the Belgian convinced the Dutch Indies government to send the young man to the Netherlands to study under Dutch artists Cornelis Kruseman and Andreas Schelfhout.[5]

The villa of Raden Saleh in Cikini, circa 1867, with its fusion of different architectural styles. It is currently in use as an administrative building of the Cikini Hospital.

Raden Saleh enjoyed life in Europe. The affection was mutual and doors opened for this talented painter from faraway Java. When his studies were done, he decided not to return to Batavia immediately and spent several years travelling in Europe, building his reputation as an artist in the Romantic school. In The Hague, an encounter with a lion tamer led to the creation of his most famous painting of animal fights. Saleh was also accepted at various European courts where he was assigned to paint portraits. From 1839, he spent five years at the court of Ernest I, Duke of Saxe-Coburg and Gotha, who became an important patron.

When he turned 40 in 1852, Saleh returned to Java. Inspired by what he had seen on his travels, he set to work on building a palace in Cikini. There were elements of Callenberg Castle, a German palace in Coberg where he had stayed, as well as a nod to Arab architecture, perhaps based on a visit to Algiers. With his masterpiece completed, in 1864 he donated the vast swathes of land that surrounded the property to the Society for Plants and Animals, which eventually led to the construction of an amusement park and zoo. In 1966, these attractions were transferred to a new location in south Jakarta where the Ragunan Zoo stands today. The old zoo in Cikini is now called Taman Ismail Marzuki and is an arts and cultural centre.

Slowly, the city's centre of gravity moved south towards Menteng and Cikini, but improvements were also being made elsewhere. For example, much further north, visitors arrived at the new Tanjung Priok harbour outside old Batavia. The new arrivals rushed by carriage through the dilapidated old city to the leafy town of Weltevreden, often staying at one of the hotels in Rijswijk and Noordwijk. The posh Hotel der Nederlanden, now part of the presidential palace complex, was in great demand, as was Hotel Cavadino, still in use today under the name Hotel Sriwijaya.

But pride of place for those with money to throw around was the new Hotel des Indes, which stood opposite Harmonie, an elite social club.

Originally the Hotel des Provence, the manager, a Frenchman called Louis Cressonnier, had the name changed in 1866, presumably on the recommendation of Eduard Douwes Dekker, a regular guest.

Cressonnier was a courteous man known to enjoy a conversation with guests on the veranda of the hotel, often with a stiff drink in hand. It seems his marriage to his Dutch wife was a rather unpleasant one. This toxic combination of alcohol and a troublesome marriage, with some opium consumption thrown in, did not end well. He was found dead at the hotel right at the peak of his career, on the same day King Rama V of Thailand arrived at the hotel, carrying with him the now-famous elephant statue that is currently on display at the front entrance of the National Museum.[6]

****

We get a glimpse of life in Batavia and Weltevreden in the 1880s through the writings of P.A. Daum, a Dutch journalist and novelist who lived in the city.[7] One novel narrates the troubles of an imaginary Van der Linden family in which the head is a medical doctor. Most of his stories were about the European circles living in the large houses and villas in Rijswijk, Tanah Abang, Noordwijk and Weltevreden. In his stories, younger men and new arrivals often stayed in boarding houses in Noordwijk, while the wealthiest had villas surrounding the large Koningsplein. In the morning, men would take their carriages to their offices, which even in the late 1880s were still located along the Kali Besar in the old Batavia town. A freshly packed lunch would be delivered at noon by one of the servants.

Daum's female characters would shop, visit friends and acquaintances or involve themselves in charity work. In the afternoon, the men would return from work to a glass of port or Madeira followed by a *rijsttafel* for dinner and an evening on the front veranda of the house. Sometimes, friends or neighbours would drop in for a glass of whiskey or *jenever* (gin) and at weekends, people would bring musical instruments to lighten up the evenings. Sundays were often used to sleep off the hangover instead of going to church. Once or twice a week, men would visit the Harmonie for a card game, enjoy a cigar, read the newspaper or just have a chat in its cool, airy, high-ceilinged rooms.

Just like Ong Tae Hae a few decades earlier, Daum depicts a high society that is highly materialistic, a place where showing off your wealth was important. People boasted about the size of their magnificent houses, the number of carriages they owned and their extravagant parties. Nepotism and intrigue were key to career progress. Many of the Dutch looked down on their servants whom they often considered lazy, naive, unreliable and prone to superstition. But some of his characters developed an affection for the locals and their way of life.

A colonial house along the Molenvliet canal, circa 1860, with the family sitting on the veranda.

On the veranda in front of a private colonial house in Batavia, circa 1917. Only the two Javanese servants look at the photographer.

Most indigenous Indonesians lived somewhat apart from these Europeans, in *kampung* surrounding these villas, often accessible by a *gang* (small alley) from the main roads. But one group of Europeans in particular developed close relationships with Indonesians – unmarried men. With European women in short supply, they often had affairs or lived with a *nyai* (concubine). These *nyai* would, just like their European female counterparts, spend evenings on the porch of the house drinking a punch. But during the day, unlike their European female counterparts, they would wear a *sarong* or a lace-trimmed *kebaya*, consult a *dukun* (shaman), believed in *guna-guna* (black magic), use *jamu* (medicinal herbs) and chew *sirih*. The children who were the products of these relationships were sometimes accepted in the Dutch circles, but more often they would find their way to the surrounding *kampung*, where they would be raised by an aunt or grandmother.

For many Dutch men, having a *nyai* was often considered a temporary affair and by the time a suitable European lady came on the scene, the

A *nyai* with child, circa 1870–1880.

nyai was thrown out and sent back home to the *kampung*. But the reverse was also the case and young European women had to compete with these *nyai* and work hard to guard their suitor from the intrigues and attractions of these local women. In Daum's books it is the intrigues of the *nyai* that often controlled events well beyond the comprehension of the Europeans.

But it is in the writings of another writer, Pramoedja Ananta Toer,[8] where the harsh realities of colonial life come to the fore. He described a world where Indonesians, even those who had enjoyed the same Dutch education at a prestigious high school, found it more difficult to be taken seriously or to find a job. Terms such as "half-blood" and "mixed blooded" were widely used. In a passage in Toer's Buru trilogy a young Indonesian man is not allowed to wear European dress, but instead forced to don indigenous clothes. Elsewhere, an Indonesian is told to toe the line and act like a "proper native" or face the risk of being thrown out of school. To many indigenous Indonesians, subjugation was a fact of life and it was not just the Dutch or Europeans who shaped this harsh reality, but also Eurasians and locals, often working in concert with a local ruling elite, who were happy to participate.

****

It was in this growing city full of contrasts and inequality where a young boy, Si Pitung,[9] was born in the last quarter of the nineteenth century in a *kampung* in Palmerah, just south of Tanah Abang. The name Palmerah comes from *paal merah* or "red pole", as this is where the city of Batavia bordered the rest of Java. In the past, Palmerah was a place for farmers who came from outside the city to sell their fruit and vegetables. Over time, a mansion, Grogol House, was built there. It is still visible today but is currently in use as a police station on Jl. Palmerah Barat III.

As a young boy, Si Pitung had shown promise at a *pesantren* (an Islamic boarding school) in an area called Kemayoran. Kemayoran was a few hours' walk away on the opposite side of Batavia, just north of Pasar Senen. This area got its name from Isaac de l'Ostal de Saint-Martin, a French commander employed by the VOC who had purchased land there in the seventeenth century. He was more commonly referred to by his rank, presumably because of the length of his surname and the difficulty of pronouncing it. As he was a major, the whole district became known as "Ke-mayor-an".[10] Later, when the Dutch left disease-ridden Batavia to live in Weltevreden, many Betawi people settled in Kemayoran in densely populated *kampung* among assorted small markets, family-run stores and the occasional Islamic boarding school.

One day, Si Pitung was robbed by three thugs on his way back from the market. It is unclear if he was scared to tell his father or if his father forced him to come up with the money that had been stolen. Having no money of his own, the only option was to steal it. In some other versions of the story it is Dutch injustices that made him to steal from the evil colonisers. But whatever the truth, Si Pitung, a pious young boy, turned from goat herdsman into local thug or an Asian Robin Hood, depending on your point of view.

This was before the days of gaslights on the streets and young men without a job would often join one of the many gangs that roamed the city at night. People referred to them as *buaya* (crocodiles) or *jago* (cocks).[11] Gang members would identify themselves by the way they rolled up their batik trousers or had a handkerchief strung around their necks. These gangs plagued the *kampung* where police seldom patrolled and where they had free reign after dark. As time passed, Si Pitung was not just part of a band of brothers, but had a gang of his own. Together with three other men named Dji-ih, Rais and Jebul he roamed the streets and alleys of the city.

Si Pitung and his gang rose to fame when they robbed Hadji Sapiudin, a wealthy landowner in Marunda, a village north-east of Batavia and not far from where the new Tanjung Priok port would rise a few years later. Legend has it that the gang, disguised as officials from the local government, arrived at Hadji Sapiudin's house and told him that he was under suspicion of forgery. They brought an official letter with instructions to hand over his money so that the local government could check its authenticity. The landowner naively complied with the request, and the gang made off with the money.

These crimes committed in broad daylight did not go unnoticed by Tanah Abang's dutiful and hardworking chief constable, A.W.V. Hinne, or Schout Heyne as he was often called. For him, the capture of Si Pitung would become an obsession. Reports that Si Pitung had been spotted somewhere were always promptly followed by the appearance of a large number of Heyne's Dutch policemen in the area, only to find out that the locals had pointed them in the wrong direction, allowing Si Pitung to evade the clutches of the authorities.

Cash rewards were offered to anyone with information about his whereabouts, but to no avail. With an increasing number of people keeping an eye out for Si Pitung, the gang had to adopt creative strategies to avoid capture. In one instance, they all dressed in an identical manner, confusing the police when gang members were spotted at different locations at exactly the same time. In the end, the police apprehended a completely innocent man and by that time Si Pitung had slipped through their fingers again.

But one can only be lucky so often and in August 1892, things went wrong for Pitung and his gang. Heyne had offered a reward of 50 ringgit – a large sum at the time – for anyone with knowledge of Si Pitung's whereabouts. The gang was hanging out in Kebayoran, a *kampung* area just south from Palmerah and Tanah Abang known for its piles of *bayur* wood grown in the area.[12] After a tip from the village head of Kebayoran, Heyne was able to get his hands on the men. The village chief got paid his 50 ringgit and the men were transported to the prison in Meester Cornelis.

Less than a year later, in the spring of 1893, Pitung and Dji-ih managed to escape from the prison by mysterious means. Legend has it that Heyne, upon hearing the news, exploded in fury in front of his mistress. Talk of the town was that Si Pitung had used *guna-guna* (black magic) to get out of jail. But a police investigation showed that more worldly factors were at play. A fellow prisoner had given a pickaxe to Pitung, allowing him to dig a hole in a wall, scramble onto the roof and, along with Dji-ih, climb over the prison wall.

But they were not to enjoy their freedom for long. Dji-ih was captured first. He had fallen sick and went to the house of an old friend for treatment. This did not go unnoticed by the *kampung* chief, who reported it to the authorities, presumably in the hope of cashing in on the reward. They promptly arrived with a group of men to capture Dji-ih, a task that proved to be rather easy as, when they entered the house, they found him sick on a bed, too ill even to pick up a revolver that lay nearby. Dji-ih surrendered and was led back to prison. But while two of his men were now behind bars, the whereabouts of Si Pitung were still unknown.

A few months later Heyne got a tip-off that Si Pitung was making his way towards Tanah Abang. What happened next was vividly described in the Dutch newspaper, *De Telegraaf*.[13] On a Saturday afternoon in July 1893, Si Pitung was confronted by a local detective near the Chinese cemetery just north of Tanah Abang. He took out his gun and the two men shot at each other, but both missed and Si Pitung escaped.

But unknown to Si Pitung, Heyne had surrounded the cemetery and his men gradually tightened the noose around the famous gang leader. Two other police assistants then spotted Pitung between the graves, dressed in shorts and wearing a cartridge belt around his waist. Another exchange of bullets ensued and Pitung fled in the direction where Heyne waited in an ambush.

The chief constable emerged from his cover and fired three times at Si Pitung. The first two bullets missed but the third penetrated his arm and he fell to the ground. One of Heyne's men approached cautiously to check if the man they had been in search of for so long had died or was wounded. Si Pitung lay still but when the constable was close, he suddenly raised his body and directed a shot at him. The constable was able to jump aside in time and the bullet flew past his head. By now more policemen had arrived and were approaching Si Pitung from all sides. Another one of Heyne's men shot Si Pitung in the back and put him out of action.

Si Pitung was arrested, tied up and transported to the police station. On the way, he received various insults from the policemen and apparently, in return, he started to sing a song. At the police station he asked for some palm wine with ice-cream, presumably his favourite drink. By now, Si Pitung must have known that his end was nigh, because he told the police officers that he would rather die there than sit in prison, a wish that was granted. They kept him at the police station and that is where Si Pitung died, at around half past seven that Saturday evening.

Heyne received a medal for his efforts and was promoted from chief constable of the district of Tanah Abang to superintendent of police for the metropolitan area of Batavia-Weltevreden. His lofty new office was located right in the middle of the growing Weltevreden town, on the west side of the Koningsplein.

In the decades that followed, Si Pitung became a Robin Hood-style hero for the Orang Betawi, who told stories of his supernatural powers and how he outsmarted the Dutch. The house of Hadji Sapiudin, the wealthy landowner in Marunda who had handed over his money to the gang, is now ironically a Si Pitung museum. Si Pitung was buried not far from his parental home, on Jl. Raya Kebayoran Lama, where a Telkom office is now located. For some time, it was a place of pilgrimage for locals and even now flowers are sometimes left on the grave.

****

At the time, stories of Si Pitung gripped the city. The gossip and rumours filled evenings on the verandas of European villas and the small candle-lit houses in the surrounding *kampung*.

Some of these people would have been my family members. There are some mentions of "van der Linde" in newspapers, but details are scant. We know little of what they did, where they worked or where they lived.

What we do know is that a J.A. van der Linde was one of the founders of a company, Linde-Teves (later called LindeTeves-Stockvis), which traded in metals and agricultural equipment. It seems that he passed away a few years after the company was established and missed out on the commercial opportunities that were to present themselves in the early twentieth century.

There is also a brief mention of an M. van der Linde, a teacher at the Willem III school in Batavia. He was given a two-year leave of absence to recover from illness and this is mentioned in a newspaper in the 1880s. But the bigger story is of the school and its students who played a role in shaping the future of education in the city. Getting a proper education and improving the quality of institutions of higher learning in Weltevreden and Batavia were topics of discussion in the second half of the nineteenth century. Before he left Java, Stamford Raffles put new life into the Bataviaansch Genootschap, the scientific organisation established in the years of Mohr's observatory. He was keenly interested in Java and wrote a history of the island, *The History of Java*, published in 1817.

A key figure in the Bataviaansch Genootschap was a man called Hoeven, an enthusiastic church minister and a fervent supporter of bringing proper standards of education to Batavia. A school run by nuns of the Order of St Ursula existed at a convent along the Postweg (Jl. Pos), a short walk from the Catholic Church and Daendels' White House. But Hoeven wanted a larger school with education standards equivalent to those in the Netherlands. Even senior civil servants could not get a proper education in Batavia; to obtain a school certificate that gave them access to top jobs in the administration they had to go to the Netherlands. Hoeven made a direct appeal to the Dutch king, going over the heads of the local Indies government. He succeeded and the funds were made available. In 1860, the city opened its first high school, Gymnasium Willem III, where some years later a certain M. van der Linde taught and asked for a leave of absence.

The school building can still be seen on Jl. Salemba where it is now part of Indonesia's national library. In those days, Dutch children would enter the school along with a number of hand-picked, talented local boys. Among its alumni were Agus Salim and Mohammad Husni Thamrin, who would later become leading figures in Indonesia's independence movement that started to take shape in the early 1900s.

By that time, Raden Saleh had passed away, leaving behind his palace in Cikini. *The Arrest of Prince Diponegoro*, his depiction of the capture of a Javanese prince by Dutch forces in 1830, would become one of his most famous paintings. Prince Diponegoro had wanted to remove the Dutch as well as some of his princely Javanese opponents from Yogyakarta. He failed. In the painting he stands defiant in front of the Dutch general who ordered his capture. He was thrown into the old prison in Batavia and later shipped off to Makassar, in south Sulawesi, where he died. Over time, the prince became a symbol of Indonesia's nationalism and struggle for independence. The Raden Saleh painting that depicts his capture by the Dutch now hangs in the work room of Indonesia's president in Istana Negara.

The Dutch were uneasy with this growing sense of nationalism. Sure enough, it would once again put the city on edge in the early decades of the next century. In the spotlight highlighting these tensions were two young people – a Dutch housewife called Johanna and her male servant, Midan.

Chapter 8
The Murder of a Housewife, Japanese Occupation and the Seeds of Independence
1900–1950

In 1914, when most of Europe was caught up in the First World War, the Netherlands was able to remain neutral and avoid most of the mayhem and misery seen elsewhere on the continent. But for four years, troop transports to the Indies were virtually impossible because of the war at sea. Batavia was, once again, isolated and alone.

Indonesian nationalists interpreted this as a sign of weakness and smelled a chance to get rid of their Dutch overlords. The authorities recognised the danger of an uprising but the war in Europe was still raging and soldiers were needed in the Netherlands to maintain Dutch neutrality. Once the hostilities ended, troops were sent to tighten their grip on the Dutch East Indies. In 1918, Batavia was city of over 100,000 souls that was like a kettle on slow boil – nationalist tensions were rising in the background, although for the moment, post-war Dutch hegemony was briefly restored.[1]

****

In a small house, tucked away on the quiet and leafy Sawo Street in New Gondangdia, south of the Koningsplein, lived Leo and Johanna Maitimo.[2]

Trams, circa 1910, making their way through New Gondangdia, where the Maitimos lived.

The house was surrounded by trees and a row of similar houses protected it from a large, noisy and crowded asphalt artery that ran along a railroad nearby. The only noise that penetrated the neighbourhood was the puffing and whistling of the steam trains that passed at regular intervals.

In the mornings, Leo cycled a few hundred metres away to his office at the administrative department of the Dutch Navy. After greeting his colleagues he would make his way up the wooden stairs to his desk on the second floor, where Leo sat in a corner designated for people of his fairly lowly position. Leo was a third secretary. It was his first temporary job with the navy and he quietly hoped that the new year of 1917 would bring a promotion to second secretary, which would translate into a permanent posting at the department and a pay rise. He knew that promotions came fast in the Far East, partially because some of the superiors would opt to return home. Leo needed the money as he and Johanna planned to have children. In expectation of this household expansion, Leo was eager to buy one of the new, larger houses that were under construction a little further south from Sawo Street in the Menteng district.

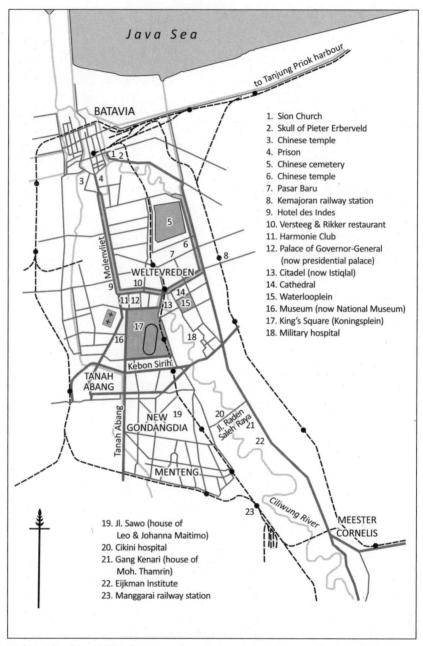

1. Sion Church
2. Skull of Pieter Erberveld
3. Chinese temple
4. Prison
5. Chinese cemetery
6. Chinese temple
7. Pasar Baru
8. Kemajoran railway station
9. Hotel des Indes
10. Versteeg & Rikker restaurant
11. Harmonie Club
12. Palace of Governor-General
    (now presidential palace)
13. Citadel (now Istiqlal)
14. Cathedral
15. Waterlooplein
16. Museum (now National Museum)
17. King's Square (Koningsplein)
18. Military hospital

19. Jl. Sawo (house of
    Leo & Johanna Maitimo)
20. Cikini hospital
21. Gang Kenari (house of
    Moh. Thamrin)
22. Eijkman Institute
23. Manggarai railway station

Weltevreden, circa 1920, showing railway connections to Meester Cornelis in the
south and Tanjung Priok harbour in the north east. New residential areas included New
Gondangdia (where the Maitimos lived) and Menteng.

Johanna and Leo belonged to the fast-growing group of *totok* or "full-blood" Dutch who, aware that there was money to be made in the colonies, had decided to leave their cold and windy home in the Netherlands and try their luck in the tropics. At the start of the twentieth century, the Dutch colony absorbed these new arrivals like rain drops on sun-scorched clay. The economy was booming and it was desperately in need of administrators, notaries, lawyers, doctors and engineers. The population of the city nearly tripled from just over 100,000 in 1900 to over 300,000 in 1920. Many new arrivals were hired as middle management of trading companies that sprouted up around town. One of the fastest growing and most successful trading companies was co-founded by a Van der Linde, and this company, LindeTeves-Stockvis, occupied offices near old Batavia along the Molenvliet canal in Glodok. The building is long gone but the mall that occupies the area now still carries its name – the LindeTeves Centre or LTC Mall.

The business boom led to a rejuvenation of the older part of Batavia. Warehouses were torn down and replaced with bank offices. Toko Merah – the famous red brick building in old Batavia initially constructed in the eighteenth century by the VOC – was used by a bank from Shanghai and the imposing Java Bank sat nearby in a building that now houses the museum of Indonesia's central bank. To provide better access, a new Art Deco-style railway station, Stasiun Kota, opened in 1929. The official opening ceremony was a big occasion for the town, with two buffalo heads buried for good luck, one at the bottom between the clock and the entrance and the other behind the new station building.

These newly arrived *totok* Dutch were different from the old, established Indies families that had dominated Batavia's social circles in the last decades of the previous century. Like Leo, these *totoks* arrived with their wives and frowned on the *nyai* concubines that their predecessors had lived with. Many considered their stay in Batavia to be temporary. As

Pasar Baru in 1936. Many advertisements were in Dutch, but most stores were run by Chinese owners.

Pasar Senen in 1936 with relatively more petty traders along the railway track, imparting it with a different atmosphere from Pasar Baru.

soon as they had accumulated a sufficient amount of money, they would book their return voyage.

They also arrived with demands for new types of entertainment. Bars, restaurants, hotels and Art Deco-style cinemas sprang up across town. An early cinema was the Bioskop Elite in Tanah Abang, showing its first movie in 1900. Popular too was a "walk in" open-air theatre that screened films at the Gambir corner of Koningsplein, behind bamboo poles to prevent passers-by from peeping in. The Metropole, an Art Deco building constructed in 1932, is the oldest surviving cinema in Jakarta. Those with small children would make weekend visits to the new Cikini swimming pool or one of Raden Saleh's legacies, the Cikini zoo that surrounded his unusual residence.

Young folk like Leo and Johanna enjoyed the jazz bars that had popped up around town. The most popular one, located not far from the Harmonie, was Blekket, its name an allusion to the Parisian nightclub Le Chat Noir, represented by a large black cat. The by-then somewhat old-fashioned Harmonie club had just celebrated its centenary and was still the place to be seen for the upper echelons in Batavian society. Johanna also visited exhibitions put on by art enthusiasts in town. The Kunstkring ("art circle"), was a short walk from her home.

The Europeans who preceded Leo and Johanna by a few years had mostly settled in the area south of old Batavia, where quite a few businesses were located. Noordwijk and Rijswijk were in popular demand and property prices had risen; as a result, people flocked to new and growing neighbourhoods such as Mangga Besar, Petojo, Kemayoran and Pasar Baru. But by the time Leo and Johanna stepped ashore in Batavia, rents there had gone up too. To find accommodation that matched his salary, Leo had to go south of the Koningsplein to New Gondangdia. This is where they, with other Dutch and Europeans, lived somewhat isolated from the Javanese and other Indonesians in the surrounding *kampung*.

****

Sometimes after work Leo would scout the Menteng area for a larger house. One day he cycled to the office of Bouwploeg – better known as Boplo by the locals – the architectural office that was in charge of the design of the whole area.[3] The Boplo name stuck and even today, a bakery and a restaurant serving Indonesian *gado-gado* carry the Boplo name. A nearby market was also named Boplo until it was eventually changed to Gondangdia Market. The old Boplo office can still be visited today, but the building is now a mosque on Jl. Cut Mutia in Menteng.[4]

There, under the initial leadership of renowned architect P.A.J. Mooijen,[5] a whole new part of the city was designed, with villas and houses along wide streets that cut diagonally through the Menteng area.

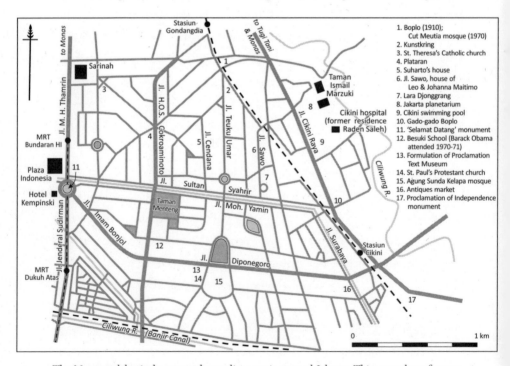

The Menteng labyrinth, currently an elite area in central Jakarta. This was where former Indonesian president Suharto resided and US President Barack Obama went to a local school in his boyhood.

Mooijen's idea was that the multitude of junctions would make the area a lively, accessible place to live. Little did he know that this layout would later create serious traffic congestion. Leo liked some of the smaller and more affordable houses near a junction where six roads came together, not far from where the Kunstkring had established the arts centre and staged weekend exhibitions. Today, the Kunstkring still holds art exhibitions and also houses a restaurant where a sumptuous *rijsttafel* is served.[6]

To execute the Boplo plan, land was cleared and locals were forced to moved further south to settlements in Karet and Setiabudi. Others left Cikini and Meester Cornelis and moved to Manggarai, an area where people from the eastern Indonesian island of Flores had settled in the 1600s and given the name of their hometown to the area. Manggarai was also where a train depot was situated. Because these new residential areas were on low-lying land, they were prone to flooding. This became evident in 1918 when the Ciliwung River turned the whole area into a swamp.

After the flood, engineers diverted the Ciliwung River. Part of the river was to flow north and west towards the sea, circumventing large parts of the city. This was the western flood canal. Another part of the river was directed further north, following its original trajectory along Cikini towards Noordwijk. There it would split again into two new canals: one towards Pasar Baru and Gunung Sahari entering the sea at Ancol, and a second that followed the old canals towards Harmonie and Molenvliet to eventually end up at the sea just north of old Batavia. The floodgates that controlled the Ciliwung waters were situated in Manggarai and they still stand there today. In 2013, the opening of the overworked Manggarai floodgates inadvertently inundated the president's palace.

While flooding was a problem for architects and city planners to worry about, the forced removal of locals from the area became a contentious issue among many Indonesians. Well-known local journalist Abdul Muis was particularly vocal. It was people like him who fuelled the independence movement and organisations that demanded more say in the running of the city. Many Betawi people felt they needed a stronger voice in their city.

The Betawi, however diverse their origins, were now a distinctive group within the city, with their own customs, food and a distinct dialect forged from elements of Chinese, Javanese, Dutch and Portuguese. But, after a steady influx of people from Java and other islands, they were also a minority in their own city and to ensure their interests were being protected, a local Betawi organisation, the Kaum Betawi, was established in 1923.[7]

A key figure in this new movement was Muhammad Husni Thamrin, a talented Betawi and alumni of Gymnasium Willem III.[8] Thamrin lived not far from Leo and Johanna in Gang Kenari, a little further south in Meester Cornelis. The area was located next to the old Struikwijk estate where governor-general Zwaardecroon had established the first coffee plantation in the early 1700s and where Dutch troops had dug in to resist the invading English troops in 1810. Thamrin spoke fluent Dutch and rubbed shoulders with well-off Dutch and Eurasian schoolmates. After he finished school, he worked for a mail company where he met Daan van der Zee, a politically active socialist with whom he discussed politics in the garden of a popular restaurant, Versteeg & Rikkers, in Noordwijk. Thamrin eventually decided to enter local politics.

Batavia had been upgraded into a municipality in 1905, which meant that the city was able to raise its own taxes and decide how to allocate budget spending. By the time Thamrin entered the city council, the bulk of this money was used to finance European interests in the city. For example, local people in the kampung still used basic wells, while a selection of European neighbourhoods enjoyed Batavia's first clean water supply. Thamrin wanted to change this but faced an uphill battle; convincing the rest of the council to allocate funds to kampung or local projects proved to be a struggle.

Villagers clustered around a water pump in a *kampung* in Batavia, circa 1930.

Articles in the *Bataviaasch Nieuwsblad* describe some of the discussions in the council. We read that on 11 April 1923, Thamrin and a few others asked for money to pave *kampung* roads, dig lined gutters on each side of these roads, and build more wells. But even these rather basic demands were akin to heresy for some council members. They argued that these *kampung* were on private land and any improvements would benefit landowners, not the city. They added that the money needed to be set aside for potential land purchases in the future. By extension, they argued that money made available to the *kampung* would jeopardise the growth of the city. It was a lame excuse, but it seemed to work. Thamrin's proposal was rejected.

To his credit, Thamrin did not give up. His eloquence, persuasiveness, soft-spokenness and persistence ensured that at least some of the funds were allocated to the improvement of roads, water supply or schools for local people. Thamrin once sarcastically argued that a disappointingly low budget made available for *kampung* improvement was a small price to pay for keeping the council's conscience clear. But eventually this uphill battle proved too much. When Thamrin was passed over for the job of deputy mayor, he stepped down from the city council. He stayed in politics and became a member of a national People's Council in 1927.[9]

While Thamrin was struggling with the system from within, others took a different path. More local political organisations had appeared on the scene. Some were more national in character, such as Budi Utomo, while others had a distinct religious focus, such as Sarekat Islam.[10] But what they had in common was a sense that Indonesians needed to have more say in what happened to their own country and their own city. To stress the point, members often did not refer to the city as Batavia but used pre-colonial names such as Jayakarta, Jacatra or Djakarta. Later, Thamrin would go a step further and ask for the term "Dutch Indies" to be replaced by Indonesia, a proposal quickly rejected by the Dutch government.

****

All these political machinations and demands for influence were playing out in the background when Leo and Johanna arrived and were looking for a new house. Many of these new arrivals became progressively aware of this growing sense of self-determination among the locals. To some, this must have been an uncomfortable threat.

On Wednesday, 27 December 1916, just after nine in the morning, 27-year-old Johanna Maitimo stepped into her kitchen to prepare sweets for New Year's Eve. She greeted her helper, Mina, who sat on the floor, crunching nuts on an *ulek* stone. Midan the houseboy was outside waiting for orders. It is unclear exactly what happened, but court proceedings revealed that Mina was sitting with her back to Johanna, who had moved from the kitchen to an adjacent bathroom to wash some clothes. Johanna then scolded the houseboy for his inactivity. Later, Mina alleged that Johanna's exact words were, "Why just stand there? If you don't want to work than I'd rather have you leave us."

Midan was incensed. He grabbed a kitchen knife from the breakfast table, walked over to Johanna and stabbed her in the side. Mina, with her back to Johanna, heard a scream. She turned to see what happened, noticed a knife on the table and saw Midan run off through the garden at the back of the house.

A neighbour also heard Johanna's scream, as did the driver of a family that lived further down the street. They both ran toward the house and eventually saw the young Dutch woman lying in a pool of blood in the kitchen. Together, they moved Johanna to a corner in the bathroom and then called the police. A detective hurried to the house and a few minutes later two doctors arrived on the scene. After a quick examination they declared what was by then obvious – Johanna Maitimo was dead. Meanwhile, husband Leo had also arrived after hearing the news at his office. The news of Johanna's murder spread like wildfire across town. The next day, a large crowd of people, most of them who had probably never even known Johanna, gathered to mourn, and at five o'clock that afternoon, her body was put to rest.

Nobody knew the whereabouts of the alleged murderer, Midan. The police interviewed his brother, who seemed to be completely unaware of what had happened and was unable to give any useful information. Little progress was made and it appeared that Midan had simply vanished from the face of the earth. Eventually, a fat reward of 200 guilders was issued to anybody who could offer information about Midan's whereabouts. This resulted in a variety of locals with the name Midan being arrested, but after a brief investigation it was clear that none of them was the guilty houseboy.

Meanwhile, the story of how a local houseboy brutally attacked and murdered a young Dutch lady spread around the Indonesian archipelago. Journalists had a keen nose for the drama that was unfolding: the murder of a young women, with plans to have a baby, right in her own home.

Meanwhile, the Great War was devastating families and friends in Europe with as yet unknown consequences for the Dutch colony in the tropics. And while many Europeans lived separate lives from Indonesians, some picked up chatter in the *kampung* alleys about self-determination. They started to feel that their way of life as Europeans was under threat, a sentiment cruelly underlined by Johanna's murder.

With the police failing to make any arrest in the weeks after the murder, the public became increasingly restless. Some started to write agitated letters to newspapers asking why the houseboy was still free. On 4 January 1917, the *Preanger Bode* reported that European housewives were nervous and the newspaper advised people looking to hire a new houseboy to first check with the local police to ensure the candidate was not on their list of suspected criminals. Meanwhile, the *Bataviaasch Nieuwsblad* got hold of a grainy picture of Midan and printed it on the front page so that the whole country could join in the search.

The newspaper commentary started to take a nasty turn and racial tensions soon flared. On 13 March, a certain Henri van Wermeskerken published a letter in the *Sumatra Post* stating that the Dutch needed to take a close look at the lynching laws in the US. He wrote that in the US, "a group of niggers that even point a finger at a white women will learn what the law can do to them ... only us, the Dutch, don't have such a law yet. But I would say, it's high time for one."[11]

The police were under extreme pressure to make an arrest. It turned out that Midan had fled the city immediately after the murder and made his way to Cirebon. It was here that he was picked up by a policeman for stealing a bicycle. Another policeman recognised Midan's face and suspected he was the houseboy whom the authorities across the whole archipelago were searching for. The Cirebon police dispatched a message to their colleagues in Batavia who sent someone to take a good look at the boy. By that time, Midan had already admitted to the murder.

Midan was transported back to Batavia. In anticipation of his arrival, a large crowd gathered at Kemayoran train station where Midan was supposed to disembark under police guard. The police had taken notice of the crowd and quickly judged it unwise to have Midan walk through a large, angry mob out for revenge. They exited at Manggarai Station instead and rushed Midan to a car waiting outside.

In court, Midan's defence was that Johanna had treated him badly. This was, however, not corroborated in statements from Mina and others who had worked at Johanna's house. They all painted a picture of a likeable and good-natured Dutch housewife. True or not, it sealed Midan's fate. The newspapers wrote that he looked indifferent when he heard a judge sentence him to ten years of forced labour in a remote part of the archipelago.[12] Depending on one's point of view, he was probably fortunate not to be executed. But the sentence still raised questions about double standards.

We don't know what happened to Midan afterwards. But the events surrounding the murder reveal a society on edge. Many people were aware of the anger building among the local population and the Johanna Maitimo case allowed these fears to rise to the surface. Local sentiment had moved far beyond water pipes and city budgets to a burning sense of injustice. Penalties could be harsh for locals and lenient to Europeans. A comparison of two similar cases in the mid-1920s illustrates this.

On 23 May 1923, a Dutch guard at the Tanjung Priok harbour, Klaas Brugman, could not control his jealousy when he discovered that his helper, whom he was in love with, was having a relationship with another man. He promptly hacked her to death with an Indonesian sword. Newspapers wrote about the *crime passionel* and considered Klaas a somewhat silly man who could not control his emotions. Brugman was sentenced to one-and-a-half years in prison. But when an Indonesian, Midan, murdered a Dutchwoman he got ten years of hard labour. In a similar case where a local worker killed the wife of a Dutch official, the culprit was promptly executed.

****

It was this legal inequality that made some Indonesians believe a more forceful approach was needed to get rid of the Dutch. Some wanted a revolution. A few self-proclaimed communists had left Batavia to plan the overthrow of the government in the safety of a small town in Java. After months of planning, they judged the time had come and wanted to inform their fellow combatants. Coded messages were given to railroad and tram conductors, who passed them to others, who relayed the messages to others across Java. One was intercepted by the police and read as follows:

> Urgent. Salimun. Pekalongan. The time is set for November
> 12/13, 1926, between midnight and 2 a.m. The people
> everywhere must revolt. All government officials and police must
> be killed. Abdulmuntalib, November 7, 1926.[13]

Abdulmuntalib's message to Salimun provided the details of a country-wide attack on Dutch officials and police stations. Ultimately, their aim was to overthrow the colonial government. Somehow it took four days before someone at the Pekalongan police force thought it of sufficient interest to inform the Dutch Resident in Pekalongan, who immediately alerted the authorities in Batavia.

Even in the days leading up to this attempt to throw the Dutch out of the country, rumours of violence were already swirling around Batavia, and the police were prepared. On the night of 12 November, a group of men made their way to Glodok prison, while another headed for a telephone office on the north side of the Koningsplein, but they soon discovered that the police were out on the streets. When bullets started to fly, some policemen ran to telephone for reinforcements. To their dismay they discovered that the telephone offices were controlled by another group of self-declared communists. To raise the alarm, the police ran to a nearby army barracks where troops were quickly mobilised and arrived in Glodok by half past two in the morning. By that time another group of communists had taken control of a nearby bank building. Shooting ensued and reports came in of more bands of armed men roaming the city. At Harmonie, the fancy club for the elite, a police officer was shot and in Tanah Abang, another had his hand hacked off.

For some time, the position of the police and troops looked precarious. But the revolution was badly organised. By dawn, Dutch forces were able to capture about 300 people and disperse some of the groups of revolutionaries on the streets. Having seized the initiative, the police systematically hunted down the leaders. By daybreak on 13 November, the revolution to take Batavia was over.

In the weeks thereafter, some 13,000 "communists" were arrested. Many actually had little involvement with the protests and attacks, let alone harboured any communist ideas. Some were let go after a brief interrogation but the ringleaders were executed or imprisoned. Many were banished to a new labour camp in Boven-Digoel in Irian Jaya, one of the most inhospitable areas in the Indonesian archipelago.

But while this revolution was neutralised, the Indonesians' growing sense of nationalism and self-determination was not. In 1927, a new national party, the Party Nasional Indonesia, was established under the leadership of a young man by the name of Sukarno. He was not looking for immediate violent revolution but neither was he keen on the approach of Thamrin, the reformer who tried to change policies from within.

Over the years, a multitude of nationalist organisations proliferated, with people such as Sukarno, Hatta, Sjahrir and Tjokroaminoto becoming key players. Sukarno was still a boy when his father, a teacher, sent him to a school in Surabaya. There, he lodged with Tjokroaminoto, a prominent religious and civic leader. There he must have listened in on discussions about nationalism and been able to mingle with like-minded people. Eventually, he met new people from a wide political spectrum, which eventually included Mohammad Hatta and Sutan Sjahrir, two nationalists born in Sumatra. Sukarno would become Indonesia's first president, Hatta its first vice-president and Sjahrir the new country's first prime minister.

But well before that, in August 1933, Sukarno was arrested and sent into exile, even after he offered to step back from politics. Not long after, his fellow nationalists Hatta and Sjahrir were arrested. And when Tjokroaminoto passed away in 1934, the nationalist movement appeared to have lost its leaders and be withering away. Not for long though.

****

On 1 September 1939, Hitler invaded Poland and the Second World War started in Europe. Germany then took over the Netherlands in May 1940, forcing the Dutch government to flee to London. Initially, all this had little impact on what was happening on the streets of Batavia. There, far away in the Indies, life continued as usual. But there would be no repeat situation of what happened during the First World War, when the Netherlands and the Indonesian archipelago were neutral and able to avoid most of the damage inflicted on Europe.

While Germany was attempting to conquer Europe, the Japanese started to send their troops across Asia. The Dutch were nervous about Indonesians who had contact with the Japanese and started to make arrests. Thamrin, one of the leaders of the independence movement, was arrested. He was by then terminally ill and would die in custody a few days later at only 46 years old. Although there is no suggestion that he was maltreated by the Dutch – it appears he had a heart attack – there were still suspicions of Dutch involvement in his death.[14] A large crowd assembled for the funeral of this highly respected member of the Orang Betawi community, who was honoured by locals and Europeans alike. One of central Jakarta's largest north-south arteries, Jl. Thamrin, is named after him.

The storyline changed on 8 March 1942, when the Japanese arrived in Batavia and the Dutch surrendered. Some colonial officials were thrown into a jail in Glodok. Dutch statues – including the one of J.P Coen at Waterlooplein – were pulled down and Dutch street names were replaced with Japanese ones. The Pieter Erberveld monument, erected after his capture and torture in 1722, had become a symbol of Dutch colonial oppression over the centuries and was also torn down. Schools hoisted the Japanese flag every morning and Dutch and English lessons were replaced by Japanese ones. To further wipe Dutch influence from the city, the new overlords changed the name of Batavia to Jakarta.[15]

The Japanese also realised that they needed to win over the Indonesian population and started to forge relationships with leading figures of the pre-war nationalist movement. Just before the war, the Dutch had allowed Sjahrir and Hatta to return to the city. Sukarno would join them in Jakarta soon after. The Japanese also paid special attention to Indonesia's youth, the *pemuda*, who responded to their message that in order to win and gain freedom, one needed enthusiasm, will-power and *semangat* (spirit). They provided military training to boys and girls, who were also lectured on nationalism.

Meanwhile, many Dutch and other Europeans ended up in one of the Japanese camps in the city. Barracks near the Waterlooplein were the first port of entry for Europeans from where they were distributed across the city to camps in Petojo, Salemba and Manggarai. Many endured terrible conditions.

Life in the city now took a sharp turn for the worse as food shortages became common and it became harder to get medicine or clothing. People started to grow vegetables in their gardens and many had to make a living on the street peddling food, riding a *becak* (rickshaw), selling soap or cigarettes. Many left Jakarta to make their way back to their hometowns, often to find that life there was not any better.[16]

One tragic war-time story involves a 1944 medical experiment carried out by the Japanese military that went awfully wrong.[17] A group of Indonesian workers were given a trial cholera-typhoid-dysentery vaccine made by Japanese doctors to check its effects before they used it on Japanese soldiers. The vaccine failed and an estimated 900 workers died.

A scapegoat was needed. The Japanese promptly accused the staff of Jakarta's Eijkman Institute for Molecular Biology, which had been involved in other vaccine work. Its staff was arrested and tortured, and one of them died. A short time later, all the staff were abruptly released with the exception of Achmad Mochtar, the head of the institute. It later emerged that Mochtar had agreed to take the blame on the condition that his colleagues were released. He was later beheaded and his body crushed by a steamroller. What remained was buried in a communal grave.

On 6 August 1945, the atomic bomb was dropped on Hiroshima, marking the end to the horrific war in Asia. On 15 August, Japan capitulated. An unexpected situation now emerged: the Japanese had surrendered but in the absence of any Allied forces, the Japanese were still in control. Sukarno, Hatta and the older generation were uncertain of what to do and feared provoking a conflict with the Japanese. Meanwhile, leaders of the youth movement wanted a dramatic and immediate declaration of independence. Sjahrir supported this strategy but no one dared to move without support from Sukarno and Hatta.

In an attempt to make Sukarno and Hatta see their point of view, some of the *pemuda* forced the two leaders to the small town of Rengasdengklok, just outside Jakarta. But Sukarno and Hatta remained unmoved. The Japanese stepped in and convinced the *pemuda* to let the two leaders return to Jakarta, where on the evening of 16 August a written declaration of independence was drafted. At ten o'clock the next morning, on 17 August 1945, Sukarno read the declaration of independence before a relatively small group people who had gathered outside his house. A museum in central Jakarta is now dedicated to the event.

The three-and-a-half years of Japanese occupation changed many things. Before the arrival of the Japanese, the Dutch were unchallenged across the archipelago. In the early years of the twentieth century, as the tensions around Johanna Maitimo's murder highlighted, the Dutch people were increasingly fearful of the sentiments in the *kampung*. By the end of the Japanese occupation, the Dutch had a much bigger task on their hands – could they regain their status as the European colonial masters of Indonesia?

Chapter 9
An Attempted Coup, Deep Purple's Debacle and a Jakarta Love Story
1950–2000

After the Second World War, the Netherlands tried hard to reclaim the colony which it had been forced to abandon to the Japanese in 1942. When Japan surrendered, Indonesian leaders proclaimed independence on 17 August 1945. Between 1947 and 1948, the Dutch launched two major military initiatives but, under pressure from the United States and the United Nations, there was only ever going to be one outcome. In 1949, after four years of military and diplomatic confrontations, the Netherlands finally recognised the independence of the Dutch East Indies, which eventually became the Republic of Indonesia.

Jakarta then experienced a period of rapid growth as people poured in from the countryside and other parts of the giant archipelago. As the economy grew, political pressures were also building, culminating in an attempted coup against President Sukarno in 1965 that led to widespread bloodshed. After the political tensions eased, Jakarta continued to flourish. This dramatic story can be told through the eyes of three very different men – Jul Chaidir, Sarwono and Adjat Sudjarat – who have one thing in common. They can all say: "I was there."[1]

****

When I visited Jul Chaidir in 2019, he was 87. Emerging slowly from his bedroom and shuffling towards the guest room at the front of his house, he refused offers of help from his two daughters and said, "I am a bit slow these days," before sinking into the large chair next to me. His younger daughter retreated to the kitchen to prepare tea, water and pineapple cookies. We had agreed to meet on a late Sunday afternoon after his regular nap at his home in Radio Dalam in south Jakarta. I started off by saying, in Indonesian, that I very much appreciated him sparing the time to meet me but he interrupted and said, in slightly staccato but fluent Dutch, "We can speak Dutch if you like but I might have forgotten some words." Clearly, Jul's mind had survived the years better than his body had.

After some Dutch chit-chat during which he told me I was to call him Uncle Jul, we continued in Indonesian and I asked him about his early days in Padang, the city in Sumatra where he was born in 1932 and attended the local Dutch school. This is where classes in Dutch, German and French turned Uncle Jul into a polyglot. At home, he was the fourth of six children. He joked that in those days male school teachers were quite popular with local women with the result that his father, a local teacher, married three times. The sibling headcount rose to twenty-one when all his step-brothers and sisters were included.

In his boyhood Uncle Jul had witnessed the war at first hand. When the fighting came to Padang, he saw the Japanese arrive and the Dutch retreat. The first time he noticed this was when, on the way to school, he was passed by Japanese troops in an army truck. He lived through the occupation, adding some Japanese to his already impressive repertoire of languages. A few years later, when the war came to an end, Allied forces, mostly Indians and Australian soldiers, arrived in town. Soon after, the Dutch tried to fight their way back to Padang and he remembers how clashes with Indonesian fighters set large parts of the forests surrounding the town ablaze.

JAKARTA

Post-war Jakarta was a city in turmoil. Different forces were moving around the city: Japanese troops in retreat, newly-arrived Dutch soldiers and youthful *pemuda* groups that were taking the fight to the Dutch, who were trying to regain control of the city. The Dutch even attempted to assassinate some of the leaders of the new republic such as Sukarno and Sutan Sjahrir in late 1945.[2] That failed but they did succeed in bringing the wheels of government to a standstill. In 1946, Jakarta was temporarily demoted as Indonesia's capital when the government moved to Yogyakarta, a much safer city in central Java. After the move from Batavia to Weltevreden, this was the second time the capital was moved.

The US disapproved of the Dutch attempts to restore their colonial powers and supported Indonesia's independence. After a series of half-hearted diplomatic talks between the Indonesians and the Dutch, punctuated by aggressive military campaigns by the Dutch to force the Indonesians into an agreement, the colonial power had to give in. The government moved back from Yogyakarta to Jakarta and the city was, for the moment, safe to visit.

Just like old Batavia, Jakarta proved to be a huge magnet for aspirational Indonesians. Once again, this was the place to find a job, make money and build a future. In the decades after independence, millions would give in to its gravitational pull and arrive from all corners of the archipelago. They often stayed with extended family members who used their network of friends and acquaintances to find a job in town. In 1950, the 18-year-old Jul Chaidir was one of them. After boarding a cargo ship in Padang, sleeping between the boxes and baggage on deck, he reached Tanjung Priok harbour. There, he took a ride to Manggarai in south Jakarta, where an aunt lived. The next challenge was to figure out how to make a living in the city.

****

At about the same time, a younger boy was also bound for Jakarta. Sarwono was born in 1939 in a small town in the Karanggayam district, not far from Yogyakarta in Central Java. There he went to a local primary school so did not receive the kind of polyglot education that Jul enjoyed in Padang. After the Second World War ended, life was tough for Sarwono's family. Before the war, his father and uncles had toiled away on Dutch plantations but in the years that followed these estates withered away and were abandoned. With no jobs and no money, the family was finding it increasingly hard to make ends meet.

Like Uncle Jul, Sarwono at 81 had a frail body but a lively memory. We met on a Saturday morning at his house in Depok. He told me about the remarkable journey he had made as an 11-year-old child with his father, from their *kampung* to Jakarta. It was a distance of more than 500 kilometres that they would cover on foot. His mother would follow once they had settled in the big city. The plan was to follow small paths in the mountains and hills along the way, well out of the way of Dutch and Indonesian forces that clashed in the valleys below. They lived off coconuts, sugar and whatever local farmers were willing to share with them, often nothing more than a little white rice with a few chilli peppers thrown in.

It was an extraordinarily arduous and hazardous journey. One day, they heard the low buzz of Dutch military airplanes coming from a valley below. Sarwono vividly remembers the moment when they first came into view. He had seen planes before, but not that close. He was transfixed, his body rigid, eyes staring in panic as the planes swooped over their heads into a nearby valley. A few seconds later, the roar of engines was replaced with the low rumbling of exploding bombs. It was not the last time that they would experience what a Dutch bombing mission looked and sounded like and to keep his frightened boy quiet, his father gave him a piece of rubber to chew on. A few weeks later, a friendly stranger provided them with a room and some food. In the middle of the night Sarwono was shaken awake by his father. A Dutch patrol had entered the *kampung* in search of Indonesian fighters; to avoid the risk of capture they quickly packed up their meagre belongings and ran off into the forest.

After following mountain paths for weeks, Sarwono and his father eventually descended into a valley where they scrambled aboard a slow-moving train. His father found him a dirty old mat to sleep on and two days later the train rolled into Jakarta. Just like Jul, they first stayed with an aunt who lived in Manggarai on the outskirts of the city. Sarwono's father soon found a job as a goldsmith and his first salary was used to purchase a train ticket so their mother could join them.

Jul Chaidir and Sarwono were just two of the thousands of people who made their way to Jakarta. Many of the new arrivals sold cooked food on the street or worked in some of the smaller shops, while the lucky ones found jobs in Indonesia's fast-growing bureaucracy, the police or the army. After Sarwono's mother arrived in the city, they moved to Palmerah in east Jakarta, the place where Si Pitung had lived nearly a century earlier and where one of Sarwono's nephews got a job at the Palmerah police station. Young Sarwono was particularly impressed by his relative's large, shiny new police motorbike.

****

Meanwhile, Jakarta was changing fast in the 1950s as the population continued to increase. In response, the city's urban planners created a whole new satellite city named Kebayoran Baru in south Jakarta.[3] Its design followed the successful template of Menteng, with houses, parks and shops built along roads that criss-crossed the area. It was particularly appealing to those with access to the very latest urban accessory – the motor car – which allowed them to commute to the city centre. Soon, the number of people wanting to settle there far exceeded expectations. The result was that many illegal *kampung* popped up in the surrounding area. Even today a cursory glance at a Jakarta city map shows Kebayoran Baru as a hive of activity surrounded by an irregular network of small roads and *kampung* that make up the rest of south Jakarta.

Kebayoran Baru was split into blocks, each identified with a letter from A to S. Blok M was at the heart of the new satellite city. The names Blok A and Blok M are still in use today. Several companies also got their hands on large swathes of land and, instead of housing, they built large shopping malls and apartment buildings. This turned Blok M into the commercial heart of Kebayoran Baru. A few decades later, the district was adorned with a large new mosque, the Al-Azhar, and in the 1980s, a large bus terminal.

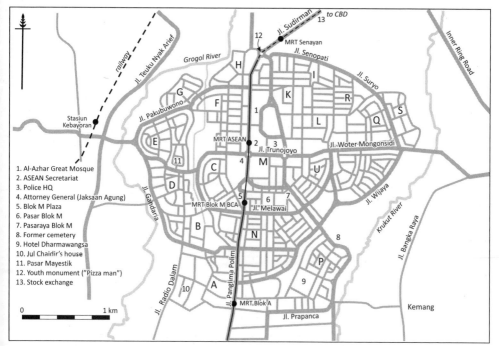

Kebayoran Baru in the 1950s, at the time just outside Jakarta. It is a beehive-like town centred around Blok M. In the north is the "pizza man" statue and in the south, Jul Chaidir's house.

By the time he turned 14, Sarwono's family was doing well enough to send him to a graphic design school in Blok M. To get to school, he took the bus. "My friend's father worked on the bus as a conductor, so I did not have to pay the fare," Sarwono recalled with a guilty smile. Despite the free commute, his design career aspirations lost out to the lure of horsepower. Sarwono's new-found affection for motorbikes, in his eyes a marvel of electrical engineering, convinced him that he wanted to do something with engines and he eventually found himself a position as an army technician. For this, he would leave Jakarta to undergo training in Surabaya. While stationed there he met an attractive young lady and a few years later, after qualifying, Sarwono returned to Jakarta, now married and renting a place in Slipi, close to Palmerah where his parents still lived.

In the 1950s, Jakarta's facelift continued at a rapid clip. The centre of activity shifted further south, from Medan Merdeka and Menteng along Jl. Thamrin and Jl. Sudirman towards Kebayoran Baru. Here, a Jakarta without any colonial context was designed by Indonesian architects and built by Indonesian construction companies. In addition, President Sukarno celebrated Indonesia's new-found independence by building many large, eye-catching landmarks and statues.

The most famous is the National Monument, in the centre of Medan Merdeka. Better known as Monas, it is topped by a flame structure covered in gold foil. The architect designed the landmark's dimensions to include the numbers 17, 8 and 45, representing Indonesia's date of independence, 17 August 1945. Thus the height of the middle platform measures 17 metres, the width of the plinth at the base 8 metres, and the width of the platform 45 metres.

A little further south, is the Welcome statue featuring a man and woman waving hello in the centre of the roundabout outside Hotel Indonesia, itself a new landmark at the time. Other statues that adorn the city include the Tugu Tani, depicting a young guerrilla fighter accepting

Jakarta's National Monument, or Monas, is often jokingly referred to as "Sukarno's last erection".

The "pizza man" is located at the southern end of Jl. Sudirman and marks the entrance to Kebayoran Baru.

food from a woman, the Youth Monument at the end of Jl. Sudirman — commonly referred to as the "pizza man" because it looks like a young man carrying a flaming-hot pizza — and a statue to commemorate Diponegoro's resistance to the Dutch in the 1830s. Elsewhere, figures in the Sanskrit epic, *Ramayana*, are celebrated, most notably the heroic monkey Hanuman soaring high above Jakarta's toll road at Pancoran. Indeed, Jakarta has so many statues that after a while their ubiquity makes them easy to ignore and be taken for granted.

To break with the colonial past, the young republic sought to erase the Dutch legacy. Street names were replaced with new Indonesian names of heroes or key figures in the struggle for independence. The enormous Koningsplein became Medan Merdeka (Independence Square), the Oranjeboulevard became Jl. Diponegoro, Molenvliet became Jl. Hayam Wuruk, and the opposite side of the square was renamed Jl. Gajah Mada, after the leaders of a previous Javanese empire. Meester Cornelis became Jatinegara, although the old "Mester" is still widely used today.

To deal with the explosive growth in the 1950s the whole city was divided into small administrative units called Rukun Tetangga (RT) and Rukun Warga (RW); RT and RW numbers still adorn Jakarta addresses today. Meanwhile, a large reservoir was constructed in Pluit, military housing was erected at Cijantung, and preparations for the construction of the large Istiqlal Mosque began, right across from Jakarta's cathedral and very close to the original site of the old Noordwijk fort.

Over time, different governors had very different ideas about how to beautify Jakarta, but most agreed that the number of homeless people, the *gelandangan*, was not part of the plan. To them, the homeless were an embarrassment to what was now a proud city. On occasions, trucks picked up the *gelandangan* and took them to the outskirts of the city. There, they were fed and offered a basic place to stay in the hope that this would solve the problem. It didn't – most found their way back into the city in a few weeks.[4]

One man who played a key role in the city's rejuvenation was Ali Sadikin, a former marine who was the governor of Jakarta between 1966 and 1977. He was a colourful and ambitious leader who, like Sukarno, wanted to turn Jakarta into a city that could match other great capitals. To regulate migration and limit the fast growth of the city, he required everyone to have a residence permit and also made funds available to improve the *kampung*. During his tenure the popular annual folk festival, the Jakarta Fair, was given top billing and staged in the southern part of Medan Merdeka. He also created designated special areas for Jakarta's transvestites, the *banci*, to roam legally, a remarkable sign of social tolerance back in the 1960s.

More symbolically, in 1972 Sadikin ordered the construction of Blok G, a high-rise designed by Indonesian engineers to replace the Dutch city council building. It was located on the south of Medan Merdeka (Independence Square, the new name for the Koningsplein), opposite the presidential palace. The position of this new city hall points to the power sharing within Jakarta: the south side of the square "belongs" to the city hall and is subject to the north part of the square, which "belongs" to the palace of the president.

****

While the city was busy reinventing itself, young Jul Chaidir needed to make a living. After his arrival by boat from Padang he stayed with his aunt and uncle. He had no residence permit and was therefore not able to attend the public school nearby, but his uncle had discovered an affordable private school a little further away. To get there, he first walked to Meester Cornelis – now Jatinegara – where he boarded a tram headed for Harmoni. About halfway he would jump off and walk to school. If he had time after class he would ride all the way to the last stop near the fish market in old Batavia, close to where the Museum Bahari is now located. On the way he would see Harmoni, the Cathedral, Noordwijk, Rijswijk, the palace and follow the Molenvliet to old Batavia. Once, passing the impressive Hotel de Indes, a man tapped him on the shoulder and told him that the movie star John Wayne was staying at the hotel.

Uncle Jul's dream was to go to university and study law, and he eventually plucked up the courage to tell his uncle about his plans. His uncle gave him the funds, on the condition that he graduate. Initially, this looked like a good deal but Jul soon discovered that while his uncle's contribution was enough to live on, it was insufficient to buy books and pay university fees. So Jul decided to look for a job. He had always been fascinated by the radio and loved listening to news from all around the world. On his regular tram rides he had seen the radio station from where news and music were broadcast. The Radio Republik Indonesia building was near the presidential palace on the west side of Medan Merdeka.

One day, he plucked up his courage to walk into the building and asked for a job. Polyglot Jul demonstrated his knowledge of languages and pronounciation of foreign words and was led to a room where he had to read something out in French. He must have done well because a man walked over and said that Jul had a good radio voice. His first job was to read advertisements and news bulletins.

"Your voice was heard all over Jakarta," I said.

"No," Jul responded proudly, "all over Indonesia and all over the world."

One unintended consequence of his success on the radio was that his uncle soon discovered Jul was not spending time at university. One day Jul came home to find his uncle in a rage – Jul had not lived up to his side of the bargain. Jul tried to make amends by giving his uncle his first ever salary but that did not work. So Jul left his uncle's home and decided he would sleep at the radio station where a few rooms and beds were available.

Jul now lived literally next to the presidential palace, just across the road in the old Van Braam mansion. It was just a short walk across the Medan Merdeka to Gambir where Jul had earlier witnessed the charismatic President Sukarno deliver one of his many magnetic addresses that held the crowd in thrall. Over time, he became a full-time broadcaster and newsreader. His voice was so well known on Jakarta radio that he was often asked to be a speaker or master of ceremonies at weddings or social events. This allowed him to make some money on the side although, Jul admits, "I am not much of a businessman and was already happy if they gave me a pack of cigarettes at the end of the night."

This new-found fame did wonders for his relationship with his uncle but Jul did not move back in and stayed with a nephew in old Batavia. In the mornings, Jul would take the tram or a *becak* (rickshaw) along the Molenvliet canal – now Jl. Hayam Wuruk – to the radio station every day. Little did he know that life was about to take another unexpected twist.

An Attempted Coup, Deep Purple's Debacle and a Jakarta Love Story

****

A complex political landscape and a faltering economy were the two dominant themes in Indonesia from the late 1950s. President Sukarno's position depended on balancing opposing forces – fractious elements in the military and the Communist Party of Indonesia (PKI). By 1965 the country was increasingly dependent on the Soviet Union and China and the PKI had influence at all levels of government. The army was divided between a left-wing faction allied with the PKI, and a right-wing group courted by the United States. Meanwhile, the economy was in a parlous state, there were widespread food shortages, and tension was mounting throughout the country.

In the early hours of 1 October 1965, troops calling themselves the 30 September Movement seized and then executed six generals.[5] The bodies were thrown into a disused well known as Lubang Buaya ("crocodile pit"). The rebels then declared that they were in control of the media and had taken President Sukarno under its protection. Later that morning, around 2,000 soldiers occupied three sides of Medan Merdeka, including the Radio Republik Indonesia building. They did not move into the east side of the square – the location of the armed forces' strategic reserve headquarters, commanded by a rising power in the military, Major General Suharto.

At six o'clock on that fateful morning Jul Chaidir was making his way to Radio Republik Indonesia to start his shift. Troops were on the streets, no buses were running and most people had stayed in their homes. When he arrived at Medan Merdeka, soldiers had blocked the road and told him to turn back. Thinking on his feet, he grabbed a lift from a *becak* driver who had evaded the roadblock and was heading in the direction of the radio station. He arrived outside the heavily guarded building just before the seven o'clock morning news broadcast. A group of rebel soldiers had taken control of the radio station. Just as Jul himself was trying to talk his way into the radio station, his colleague on the night shift was told to read out a statement from the leaders of the 30 September Movement.

Meanwhile, Sarwono, our eyewitness who by then was serving in the military, found himself also in the thick of the drama that was unfolding. Early that morning he was in Senayan, a new sports complex near Kebayoran Baru, driving a sick soldier to a nearby hospital. He and another soldier then drove an open jeep back to the naval barracks in Senen, in the east of the city. This meant they had to drive through Medan Merdeka. They approached from the opposite side from where Jul's radio station was located. "There were lots of troops on the road and no people," he recalled. When they stopped, some soldiers walked over to their jeep and pointed their guns at Sarwono. Keeping his cool, he asked what was going on. The soldiers didn't answer and wanted to know where they had come from and where they were going. Sarwono said they were making their way back to the naval quarters in Senen. After a quick check with their commanding officer, the soldiers allowed Sarwono to continue his journey. When they arrived at the naval base in Senen, everybody was out on the square in front of the main building. Rumours were spreading that a coup was taking place and that generals had been killed. They tuned into Radio Republik Indonesia to find out what was happening.

Meanwhile, Jul found himself in the broadcasting studio with an uneasy collection of rebel troops and nervous colleagues. It was time for the midday news bulletin. The soldiers turned to Jul, pointed their guns at him and handed him a statement. The director of Radio Republik Indonesia was nowhere to be seen, so Jul had no choice but to comply. He sat down, scared and confused, took the prepared script and broadcast the message that a group of soldiers had ensured the safety of President Sukarno. "I thought I would be fired," he said. But he was allowed to go home. As there were no trams or buses he walked to his girlfriend's house in nearby Kebon Sirih, where he spent the evening listening to the radio broadcasts.

The situation was still in flux. As the day progressed, the soldiers manning the road blocks and guarding the square were not just apprehensive but also hot, thirsty, hungry and tired. General Suharto approached their commanders and persuaded them to march their men back to barracks. His own troops would take over the task of guarding the square. As a result, the general was able to take control of central Jakarta without a single shot being fired.

Later that evening, Suharto announced on the radio that six generals had been kidnapped by counter-revolutionaries, that he was now in control of the army, and he would crush the insurgents and safeguard President Sukarno. After some more skirmishes, the remaining insurgents were neutralised and the coup was over that evening, at least as far as Jakarta was concerned. The next morning Jul walked back to the radio station. "It was as if nothing had happened," he told me. "Life was back to normal."

But the reality was that life was far from normal. In the months that followed there was a massive cull of communists, the supposed instigators of the coup. People were randomly labelled communists and executed without due process. Neighbours turned on each other and there were stories of landlords exploiting the situation to get rid of squatters by killing them, claiming they were agitators. The bloodshed was not confined to Jakarta, indeed the body counts were higher in other parts of Java and also in Bali. The killing came to an end in the first months of 1966. The death toll will never be known with much certainty; it is estimated that up to a million Indonesians affiliated with the PKI were killed in those few months. Suharto consolidated his power, pushed Sukarno aside and started Order Baru (the "New Order"), the term he used for his new regime. The Suharto presidency began in 1967 and lasted more than 30 years. After a sustained period of political turmoil, the emphasis was now very much on developing the country's economy.

****

Even after the mass killings, the city continued expanding east, west and south. By the early 1970s, Kebayoran Baru, constructed only a decade ago as a leafy satellite city close to the forest, was soon nothing of the kind. Jul bought a house there after he got married, close to an area where the radio station had offices and training centres. People still refer to this area as "Radio Dalam" and these days it is home to an array of beauty salons, furniture shops and a large beer garden.

In some parts of the city, the government moved out large groups of people to make room for new housing. In others, new arrivals bought land from the original owners, often the ever adaptable Betawi, who then moved further south where they purchased cheaper plots a little further from the city centre. The profits helped finance their children's education, purchase what at the time were luxury consumer goods such as cars, or improve family healthcare. Others blew it all on gambling. One of these new areas was Kemang, just south of Kebayoran Baru. Originally a Betawi *kampung* named after the Kemang trees grown there, it had cattle and cows grazing, providing milk for the rest of the city. But as the Betawi sold their land and moved on, it became popular with both affluent locals and the foreigners who were arriving in increasing numbers as the economy expanded.

The influence of these new Western expats extended far beyond the world of business, and thereby hangs a tale set against Jakarta's early heavy metal music scene, involving the band Deep Purple. The band, by then already a legend in the UK and US, was touring Asia with a stop scheduled for Jakarta in December 1975. Even by the standards of Western rock bands, no strangers to creating mayhem, the Jakarta show was an absolute disaster from the word go. On the first night, a tank was needed to get the band to the concert venue as the organisers massively underestimated the level of interest among local head-bangers. Once there, the police had to battle hordes of gatecrashers. Then things got really messy. Under the headline "Jakarta Nightmare", the 23 March 1976 issue of *Circus Magazine* described events thus:

> One of the Purple's hired bodyguards, Patsy Collins, had been
> killed when he tumbled down an elevator shaft. A somewhat
> tipsy Collins had gotten locked inside a hotel stair well after
> an argument with two roadies, and when he finally found an
> unlocked door it turned out to be the wrong one. Later that night,
> the two roadies Collins had fought with and Purple's manager Rob
> Cooksey found themselves languishing in a fetid Indonesian jail
> under suspicion of murder.[6]

The second day would be full of carnage too. With their manager in jail, Deep Purple went back into the 100,000-seat outdoor stadium for their second concert. The police, after having battled off the 20,000 fans who had crashed the previous night's show, warned any Europeans in the audience to leave their seats and congregate near the side of the stage for safety. But it was only a few minutes into the set when the wild raving crowd seemed to become uncontrollable. The police responded by firing rubber bullets into the dancing crowd, cracking skulls and ribs with rifle butts and truncheons and letting loose a vicious pack of Doberman pinschers on the wild dancing audience.

Legend has it that after the second night, the band took solace (and no doubt much-needed refuge) in Jakarta's first-ever club, Tanamur, opened in 1972 and named for its address on Jl. Tanah Abang Timur.

Even Deep Purple's departure from Jakarta became the stuff of legend. In an interview in 2010, Jon Lord tells the story:

At the airport the next morning, they let the tires down on our plane, so we couldn't take off without getting them changed and pumped up. Then they said we couldn't have the equipment to do that without paying more, so we paid thousands and thousands of dollars to get the equipment from the airport. They wouldn't let any of the airport workers do it, so the co-pilot and the flight engineer and four of our roadies under their tutelage changed the tires on the plane.[7]

By 1993, after a Metallica concert, Jakarta established its reputation as a "heavy metal republic". At this more recent concert, organisers again underestimated the number of people who wanted to see the band and disappointed fans set cars ablaze and burned down nearby shops. More than 100 people were injured, hundreds arrested and about 6,000 police and army troops had to be mobilised. Among those attending (with a ticket) was my own brother-in-law, Ucu Djuharsa. After the concert he had to pick his way through the rubble and walk for hours through the night to get home. When I asked him about his experience, he drew on a *kretek* cigarette, leaned back in his chair, smiled and said, "It was chaos. Absolute chaos."

****

But the trials and tribulations of rock bands and their fans pale into insignificance in the greater scheme of things. In the real world, forced relocations of underprivileged people were taking place to make way for new residential complexes, office buildings and amenities such as golf courses for the new elite. A little further south of Kebayoran Baru was a new district, Pondok Indah, where a developer had big plans for housing, malls and a large golf course. Again, the local Betawi people had to move out. The company offered compensation which turned out to be very low, so the residents sought legal assistance. It didn't matter. Early one morning, bulldozers demolished their houses and cleared the land. Penniless and homeless, many Betawi moved into south Jakarta to places such as Pasar Minggu, Lenteng Agung and Depok, to start all over again.

Over time, with people from all corners of Indonesia arriving in the city, the diversity of its population became a microcosm of the archipelago. These people brought with them their customs, traditions, regional costumes and culinary expertise and Jakartans became spoilt for choice. All kinds of eateries appeared, creating a generation of new foodies who knew where to get their *mie Aceh*, *coto Makassar*, *getuk Malang*, *rendang Padang*, *asinan Betawi*, *lapis Surabaya*, *oncom Bandung* or the best *gudeg*, a dish from Yogyakarta. Most of these culinary treats were easily identified by banners along the streets signalling what the roadside chefs were busy preparing that evening.

Jakarta became like a giant *gado-gado* – a local dish of different vegetables tossed with a spicy peanut sauce. As the city turned into a vibrant, pan-Indonesian metropolis of gleaming skyscrapers, a new middle class emerged, willing to tolerate much of the corruption and oppression of the Suharto regime as long as they were able to make a decent living. But not all new arrivals shared in the spoils. Slums started to appear around the city, such as Kebon Kacang, a central Jakarta neighbourhood located behind Hotel Indonesia and named after the peanuts cultivated there in the distant past.[8]

To survive, the slum-dwellers hawked cooked vegetables and snacks on the streets. Others drove a *becak* or scavenged for scrap and old material to resell. This was not something city planners wanted to encourage. By the 1970s, the street traders and *becak* drivers were forced out. The government banned rickshaws from the city and banished them to the outskirts. Meanwhile, the rise of modern retail meant that office workers started to eat in the new shopping malls, putting many of the small traders out of business. Some turned to loan sharks, sometimes with tragic consequences.

Jakarta was like a pressure cooker. While some flourished in business or found a job in the civil service, others struggled to make it from one day to another. Frustrations grew and tensions boiled over in January 1974, when a backlash against Japanese investment combined with a visit from Japanese Prime Minister Tanaka Kakuei turned part of the city into a war zone. Students and poor urban youths burned cars and buildings and looted shops selling Japanese goods. At one point, Tanaka's guest house was surrounded by a large crowd and the army had to step in. The event became known as Malari, from Malapetaka Januari ("the January catastrophe").[9]

A decade later, tensions rose to the surface again. In 1984, allegations that the army had defiled a mosque triggered a protest in the Tanjung Priok port, where the army opened fire. In the days that followed, there was a series of bombings and arson attacks, and protesters targeted the bank of Suharto's business partner, Liem Sioe Liong, the founder of the Silom Group conglomerate, one of the richest men in the country and a symbol of the income disparity plaguing the city. Another building that was torched was the headquarters of Radio Republik Indonesia, where Jul Chaidir worked (he was not in the building at the time) and by some considered to be a government mouthpiece.

****

In 1990, I sat on a train and peered out of the window to take my first look at Jakarta, a fast-growing petri dish full of ambition, hopes, disappointment and frustration. A few years later I was working at a bank in the city. Along with my friends, I would witness the violent end of the Suharto regime in 1998. The flammable combination of an economic crisis and blatant corruption by members of Suharto's family combusted when soldiers opened fire on students at Trisakti University. Massive riots broke out around the city. Again, Liem Sioe Liong's Bank Central Asia was torched. I remember standing in my office seeing smoke coming from different parts of the city as gangs set fire to shopping malls.

One evening, making my way home along the city's network of small alleys, I walked straight into a standoff between students and police. It was getting heated, and as I looked around for a way out, the situation spun out of control. The protesters started to throw the rocks at the police while others torched nearby shophouses. One of the students saw me and, still holding a large rock, walked over and smiled. It seems the young man had no issues with this foreigner and he told me to leave as quickly as possible as things would soon turn really violent. He even pointed to a suggested exit route and I scampered off down an alley towards my apartment complex. Just like the mid-1960s during the attempted coup, the best strategy for people like me, Jul and Sarwono was to keep off the streets and stay at home.

Another man who did just that was our third eyewitness, Adjat Sudrajat. His hometown was in Kuningan, a short walk from Linggarjati, the town in West Java where the Dutch and Indonesian governments negotiated a diplomatic settlement about the change in sovereignty. As a 15-year-old, he had picked up a gun and had briefly joined the Indonesian troops fighting the Dutch. After independence, he made his way to Jakarta in 1950 and stayed with his uncle who sent him to study economics at a local university. But after two years Adjat decided to quit and found himself a job in the army where his accounting skills were applied to procuring machines and components for trucks and tanks.

After he married and started a family, he decided to move from Pasar Baru in central Jakarta to a new army complex in Lenteng Agung in the south of the city, near Depok. This offered greenery and forests, a much more pleasant environment in which to raise his five children than the crowded streets in town. An army bus would pick him up at six in the morning to take him to his office near Gambir in the centre of the city. His family flourished. His sons found jobs, one of them making a successful career in the army, while he lived with his wife Uka, his daughter and a niece in the army complex where he had settled in the late 1970s.

By the mid-1990s, Adjat had retired. One Saturday morning, he took out his Dji Sam Soe cigarettes, judged to be the heaviest of all *kretek* available in the market, walked outside and waited on the small veranda. His daughter Teni would soon be picked up by her boyfriend, some Dutch guy who had arrived in Jakarta a few years earlier and who, he was told, spoke fluent Indonesian. He would share a joke with this young man and tell him that he had shot at the Dutch a long time ago. Three years after that meeting, Teni became my wife. Life had dealt me a pretty good hand.

By this time, Jul had long returned from a prestigious radio posting in London, after which he continued his career as a TV newsreader and eventually retired in Radio Dalam. That is where I met him at his home that Sunday afternoon in 2019. Sarwono, who as a boy had traversed the mountains of Java for weeks to make his way to Jakarta and found himself right in the middle of a palace revolution in the mid-1960s, had also relocated to south Jakarta. He purchased a house in nearby Depok not far from the original Depok estate of Cornelis Chastelein that was built in 1710. It gives me great satisfaction that the research undertaken for this book has allowed all these threads to be tied together.

Chapter 10

Thinking Local: Why Jakarta's *Kampung* Spirit Can Save the City

2000 onwards

This is not where the story ends, although reading apocalyptic newspaper articles about Jakarta's floods, its suffocating traffic congestion or how it is slowly sinking into the mud, one might wonder if this city has any future at all. To add insult to injury, its position as Indonesia's capital and crowning glory will soon be passed to a yet-to-be constructed city in far-off Kalimantan.

To have a future, Jakarta has to face up to these formidable challenges. It needs to confront the issues of flooding and the subsidence that threatens the northern parts of the city. But can it? And how? How will the city look in a few decades?

To answer these questions, a large dose of historical perspective is required. Let's start at the very beginning.

Thousands of years ago, a network of rivers – the Cisadane, Angke, Ciliwung, Bekasi and Citarum – wound their way through the plains just north of the Salak and Gede volcanos in West Java, depositing silt below sea level on the coast of the Java Sea. This allowed the seashore to slowly expand and over the centuries it turned into a fertile, low-lying alluvial plain with soft soil and swamps. People settled, caught fish, grew vegetables, made axes and traded cattle.

In the fifth century we find the first evidence of a city in a kingdom named Tarumanegara, located just east of what is now Jakarta. Some of its subjects chiselled messages in stone that were discovered centuries later. The oldest of these is the Prasasti Tugu and can now be seen in the National Museum.

A few centuries later, a small town by the name of Kelapa rose at the point on the shoreline where the Ciliwung River entered the Java Sea. When hermit-monk Bujangga Manik hiked across Java in the late fifteenth century and visited the small trading post, he could not have imagined that it would turn into the archipelago's main city where millions of inhabitants would settle. Even later, when Fatahillah conquered the town and changed its name to Jayakarta, it remained a small port on the fringes of other kingdoms. By that time, Indians, Malay Arabs and Chinese merchants were frequenting this trading outpost and in the sixteenth century they were joined by European traders, first the Portuguese and later the Dutch and British.

With so many interested parties involved, and all wanting a piece of the profits generated in the prosperous city, things were bound to go wrong. And they did. The Dutch burned the city down and constructed their own town on top of it. Batavia was born. They quickly discovered that the soil was rather soggy when one of their warehouses, the Nassau, slowly sank into the mud. Being from the Netherlands – home to perhaps the best water engineers in the world – they knew what to do. They dug canals around Batavia and used this surplus soil to raise the level of land in between the canals. There, they built houses, churches and a city hall. But it was still not enough. The canals could only digest a limited amount of water and after heavy downpours the city was inundated by *banjir* (floods). Not much has changed since.

Despite the flooding problem, Batavia was a meticulously planned city when it was in its infancy in the 1620s. This changed as soon as the city expanded into the lands that surrounded it. In the Ommelanden, as it was known, there was no design or blueprint. It grew organically and it was the trajectory of rivers and the location of hills and open fields that shaped settlements. *Kampung* and *pasar* sprang up near estates and sugar mills and, over time, they started to connect with each other to create a patchwork of settlements.

The exploration and expansion of the Ommelanden marked a historical turning point: the vast area of land surrounding Batavia was cleared of forest to make way for plantations and sugar mills, which changed the fate of the city in many ways. Soon, fires at sugar mills consumed the dense forests and the mills polluted the water that ran through Batavia. The rivers clogged up as mills and farms threw their dirt and rubbish into the rivers. In the late seventeenth century when wealthy landowner Cornelis Chastelein asked the government to remove some large trees blocking the river, it took days to resolve the problem. Meanwhile, clogged rivers and ponds near Batavia made perfect breeding grounds for mosquitos that spread malaria around the city.

While the Dutch may have been powerful in many aspects of daily life, they started to lose control over the people living in the Ommelanden as the population moved beyond the city walls. The social fabric began to unravel. People living outside the city became distant and isolated from the city folk. Tensions rose when the sugar business suffered a major downturn and large numbers of jobless, mostly Chinese, roamed the Ommelanden. It became an unsafe place to be, particularly after dark. Even inside the city, where the Dutch had military firepower and firm control of the government, they were still a minority, something that made them increasingly nervous. Tensions were rising and finally erupted in 1740 with the massacre of the Chinese population. It is highly likely that one of my great-grandfathers participated in the killings.

By the mid-eighteenth century, the damage was done. The city had turned into a smelly quagmire of sickness and anyone with money moved out of Batavia to the elevated, cooler and less malaria-infested town of Weltevreden. Bricks and mortar from Batavia were used to build a palace, erect a cathedral and construct new "Indisch-style" villas, a theatre, a gentlemen's club, military barracks and shops. A new colonial city had risen and surrounding it was a growing network of *kampung* where the local population made a living.

Batavia was, however, was not abandoned completely and the accounts of Ong Tae Hae show that the economic heart of the old town still had a pulse. But the mix of people had changed. It was now almost exclusively inhabited by Peranakan – Indies-born Chinese, Indians and Arabs – who ran all kinds of small businesses. In contrast, the new capital of Weltevreden was mostly European.

But there was no escaping the same problems that had afflicted Batavia. In Weltevreden, too, flooding became a regular occurrence. The new city and Noordwijk were both inundated in 1871; there are accounts of guests at the famed Hotel des Indes enjoying the spectacle of people going around town on small boats adorned with Chinese lanterns. It took until the twentieth century to dig a *banjir* (flood) canal. The West Flood Canal diverted the River Ciliwung south of Menteng to both the west and the north, finally entering the sea near Muara Angke. It still acts as the city's major defence against water coming from the mountains further south. More recently, the East Flood Canal has been completed, allowing the river to circumvent the city on the other side. Despite this, modern Jakarta still floods.

One of the keys to managing the problem is another legacy of Dutch water engineering skills – the Manggarai floodgates, built in 1919. The configuration of these gates regulates the delivery of water from the River Ciliwung to parts of Jakarta, allowing it to flow either west along flood canals or due north through different parts of the city. By extension, the floodgates dictate which parts of the city will be under water and which will remain dry. The original idea of the Manggarai floodgates was to protect areas where the elite lived, such as the Menteng neighbourhood, and even today they are guarded by police around the clock. Times have changed though, and in recent years the opening up of the overworked floodgates has been known to inundate the president's palace.

After moving the capital from Batavia to Weltevreden, the Dutch never really bothered to build sufficient infrastructure in the *kampung* that surrounded their villas in Weltevreden. In the last decades of the 1800s, Weltevreden had paved roads, gaslights and quite a few houses had access to piped water. In contrast, the *kampung* had mud roads along which people squatted around small fires. For water, they used rivers or dug wells. This practice continues even now and most Jakartans get their water from wells that tap underground aquifers. Those that can't simply buy water from their neighbours, a practice so widespread that Jakartans invented a special verb for it – *nyelang*. This continuous extraction of groundwater, exacerbated by the ceaseless construction of large buildings, forces layers of rocks and soil to compress and the city to sink. And as the underground aquifers are sucked dry, the city gradually subsides and flooding becomes ever more frequent.

Over time, another ingredient has been added to this troublesome mix – the constant and rapid population growth. By the time anti-flooding measures were put in place in 1920, many people had moved into new areas where there was no protection against the regular onslaught of *banjir*. But Jakartans are hardy by nature and have learned to live with this reality. They simply shrug their shoulders when they hear of *banjir*, while the severity of the flooding is measured by how much elite areas such as Menteng, Sudirman or the presidential palace are under water.

****

So what is the long-term solution? One option is simply to say goodbye and good riddance and start all over again in another location. Indeed, the capital will soon move to Kalimantan. This is of course not the first time this has happened – Batavia was dethroned by Weltevreden, and there were plans to move the capital to Bandung in the late 1930s until the Second World War intervened.

But some propose a completely new, counterintuitive approach. Rather than fight a losing battle against nature they want to let the water in. The idea is to go with the flow and provide room for water to move around the city by building more canals and create new lakes. Instead of its usual grey hue, Jakarta could in theory be transformed into a city of sparkling blue vistas. This idea is already at work in and around Rotterdam. Lakes and low-lying land near the city can flood when a surge of water surge hits the coast. Meanwhile, inside the city, low-lying basketball courts and a public square can be lowered in times of excess rain, to allow water to flow.

Still, despite the subsidence, the traffic jams and frequent floods, Jakarta continues to radiate a magnetic attraction; Indonesians still flock to the city from all over the country. Here is where you find the best doctors, lawyers, businessmen, artists, politicians and scientists in the country. In turn, this means Jakarta offers connections which makes success much easier to achieve than in other parts of the country. As new arrivals pour in, estates and *kampung* spring up around town, often without regard to the size of the roads and highways.

As a result, Jakarta now holds the unenviable position as one of the world's most congested cities. Some progress is being made. A new subway system is being put in place but at the same time there are ambitious plans to accommodate more people and enlarge the city. One proposal is for a huge reclamation initiative, the Jakarta Bay project, which might eventually close the city off from the sea.

Meanwhile, poorer families are being pushed to the edge of the city and this too mirrors the city's past. In the early days of Batavia, the Dutch decided that all houses had to be built from brick, which meant the less privileged were forced to make a living outside the city walls. In some cases, this created tightly-knit communities such as the Mardijkers – freed slaves, mostly from India, who had converted to Christianity – who moved to Tugu in east Jakarta and were able to preserve their identity. But they are the exception that proves the rule; most new arrivals mingled with each other and, over time, a new group of people emerged with their own unique customs and folklore with their roots firmly in Batavia. These are the Orang Betawi. Over the centuries many ended up on the fringes as they cashed in on their land in the centre of the city and moved to cheaper places further south.

So the problems facing Jakarta today are not dissimilar from the challenges of the past. But in the twenty-first century, the magnitude of the problems is very different. In 1619, there were about 2,000 people living in Batavia. The population grew rapidly to 8,000 in 1624, rising to about 50,000 in 1850 and over 100,000 in 1900.[1] Modern Jakarta, a city of over 20 million souls, is far too large and complex to move. It is here to stay. The question is, in what shape or form?

Some believe the solution lies at the individual level by relying on the initiative of each citizen. Just as *recehan* (pennies and dimes) can accumulate into a substantial amount of money over time, small changes at the individual level can also make a big difference. This approach is favoured by, amongst others, architect and West Java governor, Ridwal Kamil.[2] If one house is designed to be environmentally friendly, others can too, and a million such houses will create a greener, cooler city. If one house offers a public space to others, then multiply that decision by a million and ... you get the picture.

This idea puts the onus back on the people. The constant flooding, congestion and subsidence has given birth to an awareness amongst residents that something needs to be done and that everybody needs to contribute. Grassroots green movements have sprung up and architects, city-planners, constructors, journalists, artists, and financiers have joined in.

If there is anything this city has in abundance, it is human ingenuity. In the face of adversity, Jakartans tap into a unique brand of quirky humour to make light of even the grimmest of circumstances. Children turn floods into swimming galas, while adults go around on jet skis. To make the city greener, Jakartans have initiated tree-planting projects; one is specifically focused on encouraging couples to plant a tree on their wedding day. Others use social media to shame companies that pollute rivers. Elsewhere, residents post on Twitter to confirm the flood situation in their *kampung*, helping to map the situation across the city in real-time, a useful tool for emergency services and commuters. Meanwhile, *kampung* recycling projects collect organic waste to be sold elsewhere.

Sometimes the neighbourhood's ingenuity ensures the *kampung's* resilience. An unlikely case in point: retailers of pirated goods have been known to initiate bogus raids on their own stores to create anxiety amongst the officers who police their trade. The idea is to convince them that some other arm of law enforcement knows about their complicity in the trade, dissuading them from taking any further action. While this ruse may be legally dubious, it nonetheless shows great initiative and innovation.

****

When I rolled into the city by train for the first time in 1990, I was a young and eager observer. I enjoyed this city, full of vivacity and new experiences. People took me in with an authentic hospitality that I think is unique to Indonesians. They taught me their language, their customs, their local cuisines and told me about their beliefs, their worries and their hopes. And in the process, I came to love Jakarta and its tolerant, welcoming people. Only much later did I learn that my own family had always been part of this place. I was no longer an observer; I had become a participant.

By the late 1990s, I had landed a job at a bank in Jakarta and was sharing a house with two foreigners. Every time our rental contract expired we moved to another part of town – from Blok A in Kebayoran Baru to Ciputat and eventually to Tebet, a *kampung* in south Jakarta where we decided to renew our contract and stay a little longer. In the 1940s Tebet was still a swampy area covered in dense bush and, like so many places in Jakarta, got its name from what was grown in the area. In this case it was not the name of a tree or plantation, but the sheer density of the trees that impressed the locals and the whole area was named after the words for "dense", *lebat* or *tebat*, which morphed over time into Tebet. But by the time we rented a small house on one of the side streets, any remnants of dense bush or swamps had long gone.

It was a vibrant, bustling neighbourhood. In the warm evenings we would sit outside in our small garden, drink cold beer and smoke *kretek* cigarettes and order *sateh* or *nasi goreng* from the hawkers passing by. On the way to the office, breakfast was *nasi uduk* served up by a friendly lady who sat behind her makeshift morning kitchen along the alley opposite our house. As we waited for her to wrap our breakfast in a small package, our neighbour would come out to spray water over the street in an attempt to reduce the amount of dust in her house (and ours). At the end of the road was a small shop where people could photocopy papers, documents or even books, and nearby an elderly woman made her living selling *jamu* (herbal drinks) and giving massages to people in the neighbourhood. Her smile revealed the toll the years had taken on her teeth, but she had a stupendous amount of strength left in her hands, in contrast to the rest of her frail body. At the weekends, we would regularly drop by for a massage and enjoy her speciality, the cracking of neck bones. We all felt very much part of this small, warm, welcoming community.

Large parts of Jakarta are similar to Tebet, and to me, it is the labyrinths and alleys of *kampung* like these that comprise the essence of the city.

A few years later, Teni and I married in a wedding hall in central Jakarta, not far from the Tugu Tani, the statue of a mother feeding a heroic soldier fighting the Dutch oppressor. Our son, David Pramoedja, soon arrived, his second name a reference to one of Indonesia's greatest novelists, Pramoedja Ananta Toer (we kept the old Dutch spelling). In the years that followed more nephews and nieces arrived to enlarge the family, with some now studying abroad in Amsterdam and Kyoto. The newest addition is Darpa, a cheerful little nephew.

As a family, we all participate in small initiatives to make our *kampung* in south Jakarta a better place to live. There is regular communal cleaning of gutters, trash collection, and the planting of trees, with everyone chipping in to ensure that the less privileged in the *kampung* can get by. Young boys ensure the gates are closed in the evening, while others watch the cars parked on a corner nearby. Once a year, during the Islamic festival of Idul Adha, the more affluent members of a *kampung* distribute large amounts of meat to the needy. What happens in our neighbourhood also takes place in many other parts of the city. This spirit of mutual assistance, or *gotong royong*, is a longstanding local tradition across the city and the rest of the Indonesian archipelago.[3]

There is hope for this enormous, unruly urban sprawl. Politicians, architects, bankers and engineers must rise to the formidable challenges that the city faces. Subways, canals, roads and tunnels will be needed. But equally important are the many small changes that take place across the city, from tree planting schemes to gutter cleaning to recycling organic waste. Jakartans have an ingenuity and dexterity that has repeatedly enabled them to turn a bad situation into a much better one. It is the small improvements made by these people in the many *kampung* around the city that, just like collecting dimes and pennies, can accumulate to something meaningful and valuable.

And that is what will determine the future of this great city.

Further Reading

For those interested in reading more about the city, a list of references is provided at the end of this book. Susan Abeyasekere's book is a solid academic study of the city. Probably the most comprehensive (though written in somewhat dated Dutch) work on the city is de Haan's *Oud Batavia*, a set of three books published in the 1920s to celebrate the city's third centenary. Note that the Dutch counted back to the founding of Batavia in 1619 while the Indonesians use Fatahillah's victory over Kelapa and the renaming of the city to Jayakarta in 1527.

Good English books include a number published by Adolf Heuken. He also published a few in Bahasa Indonesia. Taylor's *The Social World of Batavia* gives great insight into life in the early days of Batavia, while Lea Jellinek's *Wheel of Fortune* does the same for life in a poor *kampung* in Central Jakarta in the past few decades. For a great English-language coffee table book with an excellent collection of nineteenth-century photographs, see Scott Merrillees' *Batavia*.

Another good source is the Royal Netherlands Institute of Southeast Asian and Caribbean Studies in Leiden, which has publications in both Dutch and English. It also has a fine library of maps and old pictures, all accessible online. The *Journal of the Humanities and Socials Sciences of Southeast Asia* – sometimes better known under its Dutch name, *Verhandelingen van het Koningklijk Instituut voor Taal-, Land- en Volkenkunde* – is also published by this institute.

Notes

Introduction

1. Batavia city archives, Arsip Nasional Republik Indonesia (ANRU), Jakarta. All mentions of "van der Linde" in Batavia come from entries in this archive.
2. Linde, S. van der. 1973, p 1.

Chapter 1

1. Zahorka, H. 2007, p. 15.
2. Taylor, J.G. 2003, pp. 15–20.
3. Heuken, 2018, pp. 10–11
4. Gultom, A. p. 1–27.
5. Taylor, J.G. 2003, p 154 and Hagen, P. 2018, p. 51.
6. Abeyasekere, S. 1990, p 5 and Heuken, S. 1982, p. 15.
7. Taylor, J.G. 2003, p. 121.
8. Noorduyn, J. 1982, pp. 14–22.
9. Noorduyn, J. 1982, pp 413–442 and Noorduyn, 2006, pp. 250–251.
10. Noorduyn, J. 1982, p. 251, verse 475.
11. Heuken, Adolf S.J. 2002, p. 82.
12. Pires, Tomé. 1944, p. 167.
13. Pires, Tomé. 1944, p. 168.
14. Ricklefs, M. 2001, p. 43, Taylor, J.G. 2003, p. 78 and Heuken, 1982, pp. 17–18.
15. De Haan, F. 1922, vol 1, p. 22.
16. Ricklefs, M. 2001, p. 34.

Chapter 2

1. Ijzerman, 1922, describes a court case of Trijntje, which formed the basis for this chapter.
2. Details of VOC ships are provided on this website: www.vocsite.nl.
3. Haan, F. 1922, vol 1, p. 46.
4. Haan, F. 1922, vol 1, pp. 46–48 provide a description of the first canals in Batavia.
5. Haan, F. 1922, vol 1, p. 50 as well as pp. 280–81.

6. Valentijn, F. 1724, vol 3A and Leirissa, R. 2008, pp. 207–213.

7. Hoetink, B. 1923, pp. 344–416 and also Niemeijer, H. 2012, p. 117.

8. Haan, F. 1922, vol 1, p. 75. The word "lijfstaffen" arguably does not always include a death penalty.

9. Abeyasekere, S. 1990, p. 15.

10. jakarta.go.id/artikel/konten/2836/bukit-duri

11. Haan, F. 1922, vol 1, pp. 80–88 and en Goor, J. 2015, p. 497.

12. Haan, F. 1922, vol 1, p. 83 and Heuken, A. 1982, p. 26.

13. Goor, J. 2015, pp. 498–499.

14. Ijzerman, 1922. It is in this letter that Trijntje describes her life and businesses.

15. Heuken, A. 1982, p. 25.

16. Leupe, P.A. 1968, p. 124.

17. jakarta.go.id/artikel/konten/1497/jagur-si

18. Valentijn, F. 1724, vol 3A.

Chapter 3

1. Details of VOC ships are provided on this website: www.vocsite.nl.

2. Peters, N. 2019, p. 15.

3. Breen, J. 1908, pp. 145–148 describes the (short) life of Rembrandt's descendants in Batavia.

4. www.jakarta.go.id/artikel/konten/3799/pluit

5. Taylor, J.G. 1983, pp. 33–42 describes smuggling, promotions and the formation of local Indies clans and the role of women in these clans.

6. Taylor, J. G. 1983, p. 39.

7. Schotel, G. D. J. 1868, pp. 307–310.

8. Kanumoyoso, B. 2011 and De Haan, F. 1922, vol 1, chapter VIII, pp. 373–417.

9   Kanumoyoso, B. 2011, p. 24, Stapel, F. 1939, vol 3, H9 and Niemeijer, H. 2012, chapter 5.

10. Blusse, L. 1986, p. 179.

11. Choudhury, M. 2014, pp. 901–910, Kwisthout, 2018, p. 11 and Haan, F. 1917.

12. Tan, R. H. 2016.

13. Haan, F. 1922, p. 136.

14. Haan, F. 1922, p. 388.

15. Pancoran Tea House (booklet).

16. Peters, N. 2019, p. 25.

17. jakarta.go.id/artikel/konten/3717/petojo

18. Betawi, Lembaga Kebudayaan, 2019.
19. Peters, N. 2019, p. 41.

Chapter 4

1. Heuken, 1982, p 24 and Haan, F. 1922, pp. 228–230.
2. The story of Erberveld is based on Yamamoto, M. 2003, pp. 109–143 and Horton, W. B. 2003.
3. Stapel, F. 1939, vol 4, p. 81, Dutch-English translation by the author.
4. Stapel, F. 1939, vol 4, p. 82 and Heuken, 1982, pp. 81–82. The translation by Heuken is shown here.
5. Archief van de Evangelische or Protestantse kerk te Batavia, letters from the Church in Banda to Batavia related to the death of Hendrik van der Linde, 1683.
6. Brug, P. 1994 and H. van der. 1997, p. 118.
7. A lot is written about malaria and diseases in Batavia. Probably the best work on this topis is Brug, P. 1994. Also see Abeyasekere, S. 1990, pp. 39–40 and Haan, F. 1922, vol 2, p. 340.
8. This is a quote from John Crawfurd in "Dictionaries of the Indian islands", as quoted in Heuken, 1982, pp. 143–144.
9. Heuken, 1982, pp. 139–141.
10. Hoetink, B. 1918, pp. 448–518.
11. jakarta.go.id/artikel/konten/4947/toko-merah
12. This refers to a quote from Schwartz in "Reise in Ost-Indien" from 1751 in Blusse, L. 1986, p. 95.
13. Blusse, L. 1986, p. 95.
14. Historians such as Crawfurd, Raffles, Hoetink and De Haan have all tried to explain the occurance of the Chinese massacre of 1740 in various ways. For an overview, see Blusse, L. 1986, p. 89.

Chapter 5

1. Captain Cook's Journal, entry for 26 December 1770.
2. Stavinoris, 1793, p. 223.
3. Stavinoris, 1793, p. 224.
4. Visser, H. 1986, pp. 123–127.
5. Menghong, C. 2011 and Jones, E. 2010.
6. Wade, G. 2007. Various court cases can be read in this book. This case is in Appendix 1, case no 2.
7. Heuken, 1982, p. 93.

8. Wall, V. vol 1, p. 55.

9. Kowner, R. 2011 and Heuken, 1982, p. 99. Heuken has a different spelling for Miero's original name.

10. Most *pasar* (markets) were initially called after the day on which they were held. But after the English left in 1815 and the Dutch returned, markets were open all days of the week, but continued to use their week day names – jakarta.go.id/artikel/konten/4372/sejarah-nama-nama-pasar-di-jakarta

11. The growth of Indies clans and social relations in Batavia is described in Taylor, J. 1983, chapter 4, p. 78 onwards.

12. Taylor, J. 1983, pp. 88–89. See also Zuidervaart, H. 2004, pp. 1–33. More generally on the development of science, see Boomgaard, P. 2006, pp. 191–217. Details on Mohr are on p. 197.

13. A history of this square and its names is in Heuken 2008. Also Haan, F. 1922, pp. 415–416.

14. Wall, 1917

15. jakarta.go.id/artikel/konten/3540/pecenongan. De Haan, 1922, vol 1 states that the name comes from drosserpad and was commonly used by slaves to escpate the city.

16. The case of Tjindra is based on Jones, E. 2010 and Nationaal Archief in The Hague, VOC archives 1.04.18.03; inventory numners 11963 (1775), 11965 (1777), and 11965 and 11972 (1787).11972

Chapter 6

1. Jan Pondard did live in Batavia, but the only factual knowledge we have of him are two newspaper advertisements mentioned elsewhere in the chapter.

2. Anrooy, F. van. 1991, p. 19 mentioned that he wanted to build an army of 24,5000 men. Ricklef, M. 2002, p. 146 mentions 18,000.

3. Anrooy, F. van. 1991, pp. 71–76 gives a whole description of the "Groote Postweg" as this highway was known.

4. Anrooy, F. van. 1991, p. 22. Even before arrival in Batavia, Daendels had received instructions to either improve living conditions in Batavia or, if he would not succeed in this matter, to move the capital elsewhere.

5. Wall, V. vol 1, pp. 24–26.

6. Heuken, 1982, pp. 147–148.

7. Government of Jakarta – https://jakarta.go.id/artikel/konten/3558/pejambon

8. Heuken, 1982, pp. 160–163.

9. Hannigan, T. 2015, Kindle edition, location 2426.

10. Ricklefs, M. 2001, p. 148.

11. Ricklefs, M. 2001, p. 150.

12. Java Gazette, 22 July 1813.

13. Mobron, J. 2011, p. 18.

14. Mobron, J. 2012, p. 22.

15. Mobron, J. 2013, p. 16.

16. Bataviasche Courant, 4 December 1819, "Advertentie"

17. Javaansche Courant, 1 December 1841, advertisment (in Dutch, translated into English by the author).

18. Javaansche Courant, 2 December 1820.

19. Bataviasche Courant, 16 August 1826, "zeetijdingen".

20. De Haan, vol 1, p. 319.

21. Niemeijer, H. 2012, chapter 22.

22. Bataviasche Courant, 21 June 1823.

23. Wang, 1850, p. 4.

24. Wang, 1850, p. 6.

25. Wang, 1850, p. 6.

26. Wang, 1850, p. 7.

27. Heuken, 1982, p. 149.

28. Wall, V. vol 1, p. 55.

29. Peters, N. 2019, p. 46.

Chapter 7

1. Feenberg, A. 1997, pp. 817–835.

2. Wielenga, F. 2017 pp. 272–280.

3. Heuken, 2001. The University of Leiden has, in its KILTV collection, a map titled "Kaart van de Ommelanden van Batavia", map number "DE 17,12" which details the Ommelanden and the Minting creek. It is also visible in Heuken's 2001 book on Menteng, p. 16.

4. Jakarta government – www.jakarta.go.id

5. Abeyasekere, S. 1990, p. 66 and Ricklef, M. 2002, p. 164.

6. Gelink, 1948, commentary in the chapter "een kijkje in Hotel des Indes ruim 50 jaar geleden". De Haan also mentions this owner of the hotel in vol 1.

7. Daum, 1997.

8. Schultz, D. 2002, pp. 143–175.

9. Till, M. 1996, pp. 461–482.

10. Jakarta government – www.jakarta.go.id. The encyclopedia has details, in Bahasa Indonesia, about some origins of names in Jakarta.

11. Abeyasekere, S. 1990, p. 67.

12. Jakarta government – www.jakarta.go.id.

206

JAKARTA

13. De Telegraaf, 17 November 1893. It describes in considerable detail the capture of Si Pitung, but from a Dutch perspective.

Chapter 8

1. Abeyasekere, S. 1990, pp. 133–138.
2. This chapter is based on a murder case as related in various newspaper articles. One is an article "De moordzaak Maitimo" in "Het nieuws van den dag voor Nederlandsch-Indië" on 7 April 1917. Another article is "Een vreeselijke moord" in "Het nieuws van den dag voor Nederlandsch-Indië" on 27 December 1916. An additional source for this chapter has been Loo, V. 2017.
3. Heuken, A. 2001, p. 22.
4. Heuken, A. 2001, pp. 70–71.
5. Heuken, A. 2001, p. 20.
6. Heuken, A. 2001, p. 66.
7. Ricklefs, M. 2001, p. 236.
8. UP Museum Joang 45, 2013.
9. Ricklefs, M. 2001, p. 242.
10. Burgers, H. 2010, p. 231.
11. Loo, V. 2017, as well as "Nu Indie", De Sumatra Post, 13 March 1917.
12. "Midan gearresteerd", Bataviaasch Nieuwsblad 23 January 1917.
13. McVey, R. 2006, p. 342. The remainder of that chapter also served as the basis for the description of the November 1926 attack in Jakarta.
14. Ricklefs, M. 2001, p. 243.
15. Abeyasekere, S. 1990, pp. 133–138 and Rickleff, M. 2002, p. 250.
16. Abeyasekere, S. 1990, p. 141.
17. Stone, R. 2010, pp. 30–31.

Chapter 9

1. This chapter is the result of interviews with long-time residents of Jakarta. This chapter depicts the interviews with Chaidar, Jul and Hardjoupatmo, Sarwono.
2. Vletter, M. 1997, p. 82.
3. Vletter, M. 1997, p. 97 and Heuken, 2016, pp. 171–173.
4. Abeyasekere, S. 1990, p. 198.
5. Ricklefs, M. 2001, pp. 338–341. There are still various stories circulating about what happened on the night of 30 September 1965. Ricklefs writes: "What happened on that night and the following days is reasonably clear. But complicated

and sometimes partisan arguments continue over who masterminded the events and what manoeuvres lay behind them."

6. Crescenti, P. 1976.

7. Lord, J. This is a transcription of part of an interview on www.youtube.com/watch?v=C1Qn02t2j7g.

8. Jellinek, L. 1991, pp. 10–22. The book analyses changes in Kebon Kacang in central Jakarta from 1950 onwards.

9. Ricklefs, M. 2001, p. 362.

Chapter 10

1. Caljouw, M. 2005, pp. 454–484.

2. Kusno, A. 2013, p. XV.

3. Suwignyo, A. 2019.

Reference List

ARCHIVES

Batavia City Archives, Arsip Nasional Republik Indonesia (ANRU), Jakarta.

VOC Archives, Nationaal Archief Den Haag, The Hague.

NEWSPAPER ARTICLES

"Batavia en Mr. Cornelis." *Bataviaasch Nieuwsblad,* 27 December 1916.

"Bijvoegsel." *Javasche Courant,* 1 December 1841.

"Brand." *Javasche Courant,* 23 December 1841.

"De beruchte Pitoeng." *De Telegraaf,* 17 November 1893.

"De moordzaak Maitimo." *Het nieuws van den dag voor Nederlandsch-Indië,* 7 April 1917.

"De relletjes nabij Batavia." *Bataviaasch Nieuwsblad,* 13 November 1926.

Dewanti A. Whardani. "Dharma Bhakti Temple to be rebuilt soon." *The Jakarta Post,* 6 January 2016.

"Een vreeselijke moord." *Het nieuws van den dag voor Nederlandsch-Indië,* 27 December 1916.

"Het Communistisch oproer te Java." *Het nieuws van den dag voor Nederlandsch-Indië,* 15 November 1926.

"Het communistisch oproer te Java." *De Telegraaf,* 18 November 1926.

"Het communistisch oproer te Java." *Het nieuws van den dag voor Nederlandsch-Indië,* 17 November 1927.

"Midan gearresteerd." *Bataviaasch Nieuwsblad,* 23 January 1917.

"Midan." *Bataviaasch Nieuwsblad,* 24 January 1917.

Newsdesk. "Gallows humor: How Indonesians cope with flood." *The Jakarta Post,* 3 January 2020.

"Nu Indie." *De Sumatra Post,* 13 March 1917.

"Publicatie." *Bataviasche Koloniale Courant,* 2 March 1810.

"Telegrammen." *De Sumatra Post,* 28 March 1917.

"Van den dag." *De Preanger-bode,* 4 January 1917.

BOOKS, PERIODICALS AND OTHER SOURCES

Abeyasekere, Susan. *Jakarta A History.* Singapore: Oxford University Press, 1990.

Allen, Saul William. "Having Change and Making Change: Muslim Moral Transformations in Post- Suharto Jakarta, Indonesia." Thesis, University of Michigan, 2015.

Alwi, Shahab. *Betawi: Queen of the East.* Jakarta: Penerbit Republika, 2004.

Anrooy, F. van. *Herman Willem Daendels, 1762-1818: Geldersman, patriot, Jacobijn, generaal, hereboer, maarschalk, gouverneur van Hattem naar St. George de Mina.* Utrecht: Matrijs, 1991.

Aprilia, Aretha, Tetsuo Tezuka and Gert Spaargaren. "Household Solid Waste Management in Jakarta, Indonesia: A Socio-Economic Evaluation." (2012) https://www.intechopen.com/books/waste-management-an-integrated-vision/household-solid-waste-management-in-jakarta-indonesia-a-socio-economic-evaluation

Bakker, Eshrin and Saentaweesook, Katie. "Jakarta through Poetry." In *Cities Full of Symbols: A Theory of Urban Space and Culture*, edited by Nas, Peter J. M., 217–41. Leiden: Leiden University Press, 2011.

Barros, João de. *Décadas da Ásia.* Decade IV, book 1, chapter 3, 1552: 77.

Betawi, Lembaga Kebudayaan. "Materi Workshop Budaya Betawi." Jakarta: Lembaga Kebudayaan Betawi. Presentation on 4 December 2019.

Betawi, Lembaga Kebudayaan. *Betawi Culture.* Interview by the author on 17 January 2020.

Blusse, Leonard. "Batavia, 1619-1740: The Rise and Fall of a Chinese Colonial Town." *Journal of Southeast Asian Studies* 12.1 (1981): 159-178. JSTOR. http://www.jstor.org/stable/20070419.

Blusse, Leonard. *Bitter Bonds: A Colonial Divorce Drama of the Seventeenth Century.* Translated by Dianna Webb. Princeton: Markus Wiener Publishers, 2007.

Blusse, Leonard. *Strange Company: Chinese Settlers, Mestizo Women and the Dutch in VOC Batavia.* Dordrecht: Foris Publications, 1986.

Boomgaard, Peter. "The making and unmaking of tropical science: Dutch research on Indonesia, 1600-2000." *Journal of the Humanities and Social Sciences of Southeast Asia* 2006: 191–217.

Bosma, Ulbe and Raben, Remco. *Being "Dutch" in the Indies: A History of Creolisation and Empire 1500-1920.* Translated by Wendie Shaffer. Singapore: NUS Press, 2008.

Boudewijn, Petra. "'You Must Have Inherited This Trait from Your Eurasian Mother': The Representation of Mixed-race Characters in Dutch Colonial Literature." *Dutch Crossing: Journal of Low Countries Studies* 40.3 (2016): 239–60.

Bower, John R. "On the Political Construction of Tradition: Gotong Royong in Indonesia." *The Journal of Asian Studies* May 1996: 545–61.

Brattinga, Maartje. "Advertising in the Dutch East Indies; In Search of a Tropical Style." *Wimba, Journal Komunikasi visual & multimedia* 2014: 1–20.

Breen, Joh. C. "Rembrandt's verwanten in Oost-Indie." *Oud Holland* 26.3 (1908): 145–48. JSTOR. www.jstor.org/stable/42722024.

Brug, P. H. van der. "Malaria in Batavia in the 18th century." *Tropical Medicine and International Health* 2.9 (1997): 892-902.

Brug, P.H. van der. *Malaria en malaise: De VOC in Batavia in de achttiende eeuw.* Amsterdam: De Bataafsche Leeuw, 1994.

Reference List

Burgers, Herman. "De Indonesische nationale beweging: Indonesie van kolonie to nationale staat." *De garoeda en de ooievaar*. Leiden: KITLV Uitgeverij, 2010. 151–274.

Caljouw, Mark, Peter J.M Nas and Pratiwo. "Flooding in Jakarta: Towards a blue city with improved water management." *Journal of the Humanities and Social Sciences of Southeast Asia* 2005: 454–84.

Carey, Peter. "Daendels and the Sacred Space of Java, 1808-11: Public Relations, Uniforms and the Postweg." Presentation on 23 March 2013. Nijmegen: Vantilt, 2013.

Castles, Lance. "The Thenic Profile of Djakarta." *Indonesia* 1 (1967): 153–204.

Chaidar, Jul, in discussion with the author, 19 January 2020.

Chijs, J.A. van der (ed.). *Nederlandsch-Indisch Plakkaatboek 1602–1811*. 17 vols. Batavia and 's-Gravenhage: M Nijhoff ('s Gravenhage) and Landsdrukkerij (Batavia), 1885–1901.

Chijs, J.A. van der (ed.). *Dahregister gehouden int Casteel Batavia vant passerende daer ter plaetse als over geheel Nederlants-India*. 31 vols. Batavia and 's-Gravenhage, 1881–1931.

Choudhury, Manilata. "Mardijkers of Batavia: Construction of a colonial identity (1619–1650)." *Proceedings of the Indian History Congress*. India History Congress, 2014. 901–10.

Cobban, James L. "The Ephemeral Historic District in Jakarta." *Geographical Review* 7.3 (1985): 300–18.

Columbijn, F. "Explaining the Violent Solution in Indonesia." *The Brown Journal of World Affairs* 2002: 49–56.

Columbijn, F. "Global and local perspectives on Indonesia's environmental problems and the role of NGO's." *Journal of the Humanities and Social Sciences of Southeast Asia* 01 January 1998: 305–34.

Conradi, Petrus. *Batavia, de hoofdstad van Neêrlands O. Indien [...] beschreeven*. Amsterdam: Volkert van der Plaats, 1768–1801, 1782.

Cook, James. *Captain Cook's Journal during his first voyage round the world made in H.M. Bark "Endeavour" 1768-71: A Literal Transcription of the Original Mss.with Notes and Introduction*, edited by Captain W.J.L. Wharton. https://ebooks.adelaide.edu.au/c/cook/james/c77j/index.html

Crawfurd, John. *A Descriptive Dictionary of the Indian islands & Adjacent Countries*. London: Bradbury & Evans, 1856.

Crescenti, Peter. "Jakarta nightmare." *Circus Magazine,* issue 129 (1976).

Daum, P.A. *Verzamelde romans*. Vols 1–3, edited by Gerard Termorshuizen. Amsterdam : Nijgh & van Ditmar, 1997.

De Graaf, dr. H.J. "De Regering van Sultan Agung, Vorst van Mataram 1613-1645, en die van zijn voorganger Panebahan Seda-Ing-Krapjak 1601-1613." *Verhandelingen van het Koningklijk Instituut voor Taal-, Land- en Volkenkunde* (1958).

de la Croix, Humphrey, et al. *Indie herinnert en beschouwd: Sociale geschiedenis van een kolonie (1930–1957)*. Amsterdam: KJBB, 1997.

Dharmowijono, W. *Van Koelies, klontongs en kapiteins: het beeld van der Chinezen in Indisch-Nederlands literair proza 1880–1950*. PhD thesis. Amsterdam: Universiteit Amsterdam, 2009.

Dinas Komunikasi, Informatika dan Statistik Pemprov DKI Jakarta. *Ensiklopedi*. 1995–2020. 2019. https://jakarta.go.id.

Djoko Soekiman and Bambang Purwanto. "The Indis Style: The Transformation and Hybridization of Buildings Culture in Colonial Java Indonesia." *Paramita: Historical Studies Journal* 2018: 137–51.

Ehrich, Kami. *Tales of Old Batavia: Treasures from the Big Durian*. Hong Kong: Earnshaw Books Ltd, 2015.

Elissa, Evawani. *The Recreational Landscape of Weltevreden Since Indonesian Colonization*. Universitas Indonesia, 2018. http://www.cujucr.com/downloads/Individual%20Articles/17/vol17%20Evawani%20Ellisa.pdf

Erwantoro, Heru. *Hari jadi Kota Jakarta*. Bandung: Balai Pelestarian Sejarah dan Nilai Tradisional Bandung, 2009.

Farnham, Dawn. *The Shallow Seas: A Tale of Two Cities: Singapore and Batavia*. Singapore: Monsoon Books, 2015.

Feenberg, Anne-Marie. ""Max Havelaar": An Anti-Imperialist Novel." *MLN* 112.5 (1997): 817–35.

Gelink, J.M.B., et al. *50 jaar N.V. Hotel des Indes Batavia*. Batavia, 1948.

Goor, Jur van. *Jan Pieterszoon Coen 1587-1629; Koopman-koning in Azie*. Amsterdam: Uitgeverij Boom, 2015.

Gooszen, Dr. A. J. "Population census in VOC-Batavia, 1673–1792." 2000.

Graaf, H.J. "Tomé Pires' ,,Suma Oriental" en het tijdperk van godsdienstovergang op Java." *Journal of the Humanities and Social Sciences of Southeast Asia* 108.2 (1952): 132–171.

Grijns, Kees and Nas, Peter J.M., eds. *Jakarta-Batavia: Socio-cultural essays*. Leiden: KITLV Press, 2000.

Gultom, Annissa. "Kalapa – Jacatra –Batavia - Jakarta: An old city that never gets old." *Journal of Archaeology and Fine Arts in Southeast Asia* (2017): 1–27.

Gunawan, Juniati and Semerdanta Pusaka. "Introducing the Urban Metabolism Approach for a Sustainable City: A Case of Jakarta, Indonesia." *Journal of Applied Management Accounting Research* 14, no. 1 (2016).

Gunn, Geoffrey C. *History Without Borders: The Making of an Asian World Region, 1000-1800*. Hong Kong: Hong Kong University Press, 2011.

Gusman J. Nawi. *Mengenang Landhuis Pondok Gede*. 9 May 2019.

Haan, dr. F. de. *Oud Batavia*. 2 vols. Batavia: Kolff, 1922.

Haan, dr. F. de. "De Laatste der Mardijkers." *Journal of the Humanities and Social Sciences of Southeast Asia* 73, no. 1 (1917).

Reference List

Hagen, Piet. *Koloniale oorlogen in Indonesie; vijf eeuwen verzet tegen vreemde overheersing*. Amsterdam, Antwerpen: Uitgeverij de Arbeiderspers, 2018.

Hannigan, Tim. *A Brief History of Indonesia: Sultans, Spices, and Tsunamis: The Incredible Story of Southeast Asia's Largest Nation*. Tokyo, Rutland (Vermont) and Singapore: Tuttle Publishing, 2015.

Hardjosupatmo, Sarwono, in discussion with the author, 18 January 2020.

Heuken, Adolf S.J. and Grace Pamungkas. *Menteng, "Kota taman" pertama di Indonesia*. Jakarta: Yayasan Cipta Loka Caraka, 2001.

Heuken, Adolf S.J. *Historical Sites of Jakarta*. Jakarta: Yayasan Cipta Loka Caraka, 1982.

——. *Sumber-sumber asli sejarah Jakarta (Jilid III)*. Jakarta: Yayasan Cipta Loka Caraka, 2001.

——. *The earliest Portuguese sources for the history of Jakarta: including all other historical documents from the 5th to the 16th centuries*. Jakarta: Yayasan Cipta Loka Caraka, 2002.

——. *Medan Merdeka - Jantung Ibukota RI*. Jakarta: Yayasan Cipta Loka caraka, 2008.

——. *Translation of and Commentary on all pages concerning Batavia in J.W. Heydt's "Allerneuster Geographisch- und Topographischer Schau-platz von Africa und Ost-Indien", Wilhermsdorff, 1744*. Jakarta: Yayasan Cipta Loka Caraka and Kartini Collection, 2013.

——. *Tempat-tempat bersejarah di Jakarta (edisi ke-8)*. Jakarta: Yayasan Cipta Loka Caraka, 2016.

——. *Sejarah Jakarta dalam lukisan dan foto*. Jakarta: Yayasan Cipta Lika Caraka, 2017.

——. *Sejarah Jakarta dari masa prasejarah sampai akhir abad ke-20*. Jakarta: Yayasan Cipta Loka Caraka, 2018.

Hoetink, B. "Ni Hoekong Kapitein der Chineezen te batavia in 1740." *Journal of the Humanities and Social Sciences of Southeast Asia* 74.1 (1918): 448–518.

Hoetink, B. "So Bing Kong; Het Eerste Hoofd der Chineezen te Batavia." *Journal of the Humanities and Social Sciences of Southeast Asia* 1923: 344–416.

Holderness, Tomas and Etienne Turpin. "How tweeting about floods became a civic duty in Jakarta." *The Guardian*, 25 January 2016.

Horton, William Bradley. "Pieter Elberveld: The Modern Adventure of an Eighteenth Century Indonesian Hero." *Indonesia* no. 76 (October 2003): 147–98.

Hosen, Nadirsyah. "Religion and the Indonesian Constitution: A Recent Debate." *Journal of Southeast Asian Studies* October 2005.

Huysers, Ary. *Het leeven van Reinier de Klerk, gouverneur generaal van Nederlands Indie*. Utrecht: Paddenburg, Abraham van, 1750–90, 1788. https://www.delphcr.nl/nl/boeken/view?coll=boeken&identifier=dpo:4806:mpeg21:0132

IJzerman, Dr. J. W. "Het verzoekschrift eener Bataviasche weduwe in 1632." *Journal of the Humanities and Social Sciences of Southeast Asia* January 1922.

Jellinek, Lea. *The Wheel of Fortune: The History of a Poor Community in Jakarta*. Honolulu: University of Hawaii Press, 1991.

Jones, Eric. *Wives, Slaves, and Concubines : A History of the Female Underclass in Dutch Asia*. Northern Illinois University Press, DeKalb, 2010. Kindle file.

Jong, J.J.P. de. *De waaier van het fortuin: van handelscompagnie tot koloniaal Imperium: de Nederlanders in Azie en de Indonesische archipel 1595-1950*. Den Haag: Sdu Uitgevers, 1998.

Kanumoyoso, Bondan. *Beyond the city wall : society and economic development in the Ommelanden of Batavia, 1684-1740*. Thesis, University of Leiden, 2011.

Kehoe, Marsely L. "Dutch Batavia: Exposing the Hierarchy of the Dutch Colonial City." Journal of Historians of Netherlandish Art 7.1 (Winter 2015).

Kennedy, Paul M. *The Rise of the Anglo-German Antagonism, 1860-1914*. Amherst, New York: Humanities Press, 1987.

Kern, R.A. "De Verbreiding van den Islam." In *Geschiedenis van Nederlands-Indie*, edited by Stapel, dr. F.W. Vol. 1. Amsterdam: Uitgeversmaatschappij Joost van den Vondel, 1938. 299–365.

Knaap, Gerrit. *VOC kenniscentrum*. 1 July 2014. Huygens Instituut voor Nederlandse Geschiedenis. 13 April 2019. https://www.voc-kenniscentrum.nl.

Kooy, Michelle and Bakker, Karen. "(Post)Colonial Pipes Urban Water Supply in Colonial and Contemporary Jakarta." In *Cars, Conduits, and Kampongs: The Modernization of the Indonesian City, 1920–1960*, edited by Freek Colombijn and Joost Coté. Leiden: Koninklijk Instituut voor Taal-, Land- en Volkenkunde, 2014. 63-86.

Kooy, Michelle Elan. *Relations of Power, Networks of Water: Governing Urban Waters, Spaces, and Populations in (Post)Colonial Jakarta*. Doctoral Thesis, University of British Colombia, 2008.

Kooy, Michelle, Carolin Tina Walter and Indrawan Prabaharyaka. "Inclusive development of urban water services in Jakarta: The role of groundwater." *Habitat International* 73 (2018): 109–118.

Kowner, Rotem. "An obscure history." *Inside Indonesia* 104 (2011).

Krom, N.J. Prof. dr. "De Hindoejavaanse Tijd." In *Geschiedenis van Nederlands-Indie*, edited by Stapel, dr. F.W. Vol. 1. Amsterdam: Uitgeversmaatschappij Joost van den Vondel, 1938. 117–42.

Kumar, Ann and McGlynn, John H. *Illuminations: The Writing Traditions of Indonesia: featuring manuscripts from the National Library of Indonesia*. Jakarta, New York and Tokyo: The Lontar Foundation and Weatherhill, 1996.

Kurniawati Hastuti Dewi. "Javanese Women and Islam: Identity Formation since the Twentieth Century." *Southeast Asian Studies* April 2012: 109–140.

Kusno, Abidin. *After the new order: space, politics and Jakarta*. Jakarta: University of Hawai'i Press Honolulu, 2013.

Kwisthout, Jan-Karel. *De Mardijkers van Tugu en Depok: vrijmaking, bevrijding en merdeka*. Zoetermeer: Lecturium Uitgeverij, 2018.

Lach, Donald F. and Van Kley, Edwin J. *Asia in the making of Europe*. Vol. 3. Chicago, London: University of Chicago Press, 1993.

Leirissa, R.Z. "François Valentijn: Antara etika dan estetika." *Wacana Journal of the Humanities of Indonesia* 10.2 (2008): 207–213.

Reference List

Leupe, P.A. and Hacobian, M. "The Siege and Capture of Malacca from the Portuguese in 1640-1641." *Journal of the Malayan Branch of the Royal Asiatic Society* 14.1 (1968): 124.

Linde, Siemen van der. *Vollenhoofs geslacht "van der Linde"*. Zwolle, 1973.

Locher-Scholten, Elsbeth. "Dutch Expansion in the Indonesian Archipelago around 1900 and the Imperialism Debate." *Journal of Southeast Asian Studies* vol. 25, no. 1 (March 1994): 91–111.

Lohanda, Mona. *Growing Pains: The Chinese and the Dutch in Colonial Java, 1890–1942*. Jakarta: Yayasan Cipta Loka Caraka, 2002.

Loo, Vilan van de. *"She gave up after a few seconds": A sensational murder in the Dutch East Indies*. Last updated 27 December 2017. 27 October 2019. https://historiek.net/zij-gaf-na-enkele-seconden-den-geest/74116/

Loos-Haaxman, J. de. "Een portret van de landvoogd Adriaan valckenier." *Journal of the Humanities and Social Sciences of Southeast Asia* 112.3 (1956): 267–70.

López-Martín, Francisco Javier. *Historical and Technological Evolution of Artillery From its Earliest Widespread Use Until The Emergence of Mass-Production Techniques*. PhD thesis, London Metropolitan University, 2007.

Lord, Jon. Deep Purple Mark IV Indonesian Tour - Highlights from Jakarta 1975. Video. 2010. https://www.youtube.com/watch?v=KwYP8U3kpss

Lucassen, J. and Rossum, M. van. "Smokkelloon en zilverstromen: illegale export van edelmetaal via de VOC." *Low Countries Journal of Social and Economic History* 2016: 99–113.

Marshall, Paul. "Conflicts in Indonesian Islam." *Hudson Institute*, 31 May 2018.

McVey, Ruth Thomas. *The Rise of Indonesian Communism*. Jakarta: Equinox Publishing, 2006 (authorised reprint edition).

Menghong, Chen. *De Chinese Gemeenschap van Bataia 1843-1865: een onderzoek naar het Kong Koan-archief*. Leiden: Leiden University Press, 2011.

Merrrillees, Scott. Batavia in Nineteenth Century Photographs. Singapore: Editions Didier Millet, 2010.

Mobron, Jan-Jaap. *The Factorij: Bank, Museum, Monument*. Jakarta: Bank Mandiri, 2011.

Museum Perumusan Nashkah Proklamasi. 23 December 2019. http://www.munasprok.go.id

Nas, Peter J. M. "The urban anthropologist as flâneur: The symbolic pattern of Indonesian cities." *Wacana Journal of the Humanities of Indonesia* 14 (2012): 429–54.

Nas, Peter J.M. "Jakarta, City Full of Symbols: An Essay in Symbolic Ecology." *Sojourn: Journal of Social Issues in Southeast Asia* 7.2 (1992): 175–207.

Niemeijer, Hendrik E. *Batavia: een koloniale samenleving in de 17e eeuw*. Amsterdam: Uitgeverij Balans, 2012.

Noorduyn, J and Teeuw, A. *Three Old Sundanese Poems*. Leiden: KITLV Press, 2006.

Noorduyn, J. "Bujangga Manik's Journeys through Java: Topographical Data from an Old Sundanese Source." *Journal of the Humanities and Social Sciences of Southeast Asia* 138.4 (1982): 413–42.

Noorduyn, J. and Verstappen, H. Th. "Purnavarman's river-works near Tugu." *Journal of the Humanities and Social Sciences of Southeast Asia* 128.2 (1972): 299–307.

Pancoran Tea House. "Preserving Chinese tea tradition." n.d. booklet.

Peters, Nonja and Snoeijer, Geert. *Depok: De droom van Cornelis Chastelein*. Volendam: LM Publishers, 2019.

Pires, Tomé. *The Suma oriental of Tomé Pires : an account of the East, from the Red Sea to Japan, written in Malacca and India in 1512-1515 ; and, the book of Francisco Rodrigues, rutter of a voyage in the Red Sea, nautical rules, almanack and maps, written and drawn.* Vol. 1. McGill University Library digitised title, 1944.

Prabaharyaka, Indrawan. "Institutional Pathologies and Urban Water Access: A Case Study of Jakarta, Indonesia." Thesis, Monash University South Africa, 2014.

Provinsi DKI Jakarta. https://jakarta.go.id/artikel/kategori/73/ensiklopedi. 19 December 2019.

Qurtuby, Sumanto al. "The Tao of Islam: Cheng Ho and the Legacy of Chinese Muslims in Pre-Modern Java." *Studia Islamika* 16.1 (2009): 51–78.

Raben, Remco. *Batavia and Colombo. The Ethnic and Spatial Order of Two Colonial Cities 1600-1800*. PhD Thesis, University Leiden, 1996.

Ray, Sandeep. "The Komedi Bioscoop: Early Cinema in Colonial Indonesia." *Journal of Southeast Asian Studies* February 2018.

Ricklefs, M. C. *A History of Modern Indonesia since c1200*. Houndmills, Basingstoke, Hampshire: Palgrave, 2001.

Riskianingrum, Devi. "The Chinese and Crime in the Ommelanden of Batavia 1780–93." *Masyarakat Indonesia* June 2013: 157–91.

Roberts, Mark; Gil Sander, Frederico; Tiwari, Sailesh. *Time to ACT : Realizing Indonesia's Urban Potential*. Washington, DC: World Bank, 2019.

Roo, Prof. Dr. L.W.G. de. "De Conspiratie van 1721." *Tijdschrift voor Indische Taal-, Land-, en Volkenkunde* 5.1 (1866): 362–97.

Salim, Agus, in discussion with the author, 18 January 2020.

Salmon, Claudine. "The Massacre of 1740 as reflected in a Contemporary Chinese Narrative." *Archipel* 77 (2009): 149–54.

Sastramidjaja, Yatun. "This is not a Trivialization of the Past: Youthful Re-Meditions of Colonial Memory in Jakarta." *Journal of the Humanities and Social Sciences of Southeast Asia* 170, no. 4 (2014).

Schotel, G.D.J. *Het Oud-Hollandsch huisgezin der zeventiende eeuw*. Haarlem: A.C. Kruseman, 1868.

Schultz, Daniel F. and Maryanne Felter. "Education, History, and Nationalism in Pramoedja Toer's "Buru Quartet"." *Crossroads: An Interdisciplinary Journal of Southeast Asian Studies* 16.2 (2002): 143–75.

Senja, Anggita Muslimah Maulidya Prahara. "Sejarah Tanah Abang, dari Kebun Palem hingga Pusat Grosir." *Kompas,* 9 November 2017.

Reference List

Sholihah, Arif & Heath, Tim. "Assessing the Quality of Traditional Street in Indonesia: A case study of Pasar Baru Street." *AMER International Conference on Quality of Life*. Medan: Procedia, 2016. 244–54.

Stapel, Dr. F.W. *Geschiedenis van Nederlandsch Indie*. vols. I–VI. Amsterdam: Uitgeversmaatschappij Joost van den Vondel, 1939.

Stavorinus, J.S. *Reize van Zeeland, over de Kaap de Goede Hoop, naar Batavia [...] in de jaaren MDCCLXVIII tot MDCCLXXI*. Leiden: Honkoop, Jan, 1793.

Stone, Richard. "Righting a 65-Year-Old Wrong." *Science* 329.5987 (2010): 30–31.

Strehler, A. *Bijzonderheden wegens Batavia en deszelfs omstreken, uit het dagboek gedurende twee reizen, derwaarts in 1828-1830, van Dr. Strehler*. Haarlem: W.A. Loosjes, 1833.

Suhartono, WP, et al. *Yogyakarta Ibu Kota Republik Indonesia 1946–1949*. Yogyakarta: Yayasan Soedjatmoko, 2002.

Sunaryo, Rony Gunawan, Nindyo Ikaputra Soewarno and Bakti Setiawan. "Colonial and traditional urban space in Java: a morphological study of ten cities." *DIMENSI (Journal of Architecture and Built Environment)* 40.2 (2013): 77–88.

Suratminto, Lilie. "Pembantaian Etnis Cina di Batavia 1740: Dampak Konflik Golongan "Prinsgezinden" dan "Staatsgezinden" di Belanda." *Wacana Journal of the Humanities of Indonesia* 6.1 (2004): 1–26.

Susantio, Djulianto. "Lindeteves, Pabrik Baja Masa VOC." *Kompas*, 5 September 2012.

Suwignyo, Agus. "Gotong Royong as Social Citizenship in Indonesia, 1940s to 1990s." *Journal of Southeast Asian Studies* September 2019.

Suwignyo, Agus. "The Great Depression and the Changing Trajectory of Public Education Policy in Indonesia, 1930–42." *Journal of Southeast Asian Studies* October 2013.

Tagliacozzo, Eric. "Kettle on a Slow Boil: Batavia's Threat Perceptions in the Indies' Outer Islands, 1870–1910." *Journal of Southeast Asian Studies* March 2000.

Tan, Raan-Hann. *Por-Tugu-Ese? The Protestant Tugu Community of Jakarta, Indonesia*. Thesis, Instituto Universitario de Lisboa, 2016.

Taylor, Jean Gelman. "Meditations on a Portrait from Seventeenth-Century Batavia." *Journal of Southeast Asian Studies* February 2006.

Taylor, Jean Gelman. *Indonesia: peoples and histories*. New Haven & London: Yale University Press, 2003.

Taylor, Jean Gelman. *The Social World of Batavia, European and Eurasian in Dutch Asia*. London: The University of Wisconsin Press, 1983.

Till, Margreet. "In search of Si Pitung; The history of an Indonesian legend." *Journal of the Humanities and the Social Sciences of Southeast Asia* 152.3 (1996): 461–82.

UP Museum Joang 45. *Sepak Terjang Mohammad Hoesni Thamrin*, edited by Irna Hadi Soewito. Jakarta: UP Museum Joang 45, 2013.

Valentijn, Francois. *Oud-en Nieuw Oost-Indien*. Dordrecht: Johannes van Braam, boekverkoper, 1724.

Vermeulen, J.Th. *De Chineezen te Batavia en de troebelen van 1740*. Leiden: IJdo, 1938.

Visser, Hans. "Jan Brandes, Lutheran minister and draughtsman." *Bulletin van het Rijksmuseum* 2 (1986): 123–27.

Vletter, M.E de, Voskuil, R.P.G.A., Diessen, J.R. van. *Batavia / Djakarta / Jakarta: Beeld van een metamorphose.* Purmerend: Asia Maior, 1997.

Voskuil, R.P.G.A, et al. *Bandoeng: beeld van een stad.* Purmerend: Asia Maior, 1999.

Voskuil, R.P.G.A. *Batavia: beeld van een stad.* Houten: Fibula, 1989.

Wade, Geoff. "Chinese Economic Activities in Java in the Late Eighteenth Century as Reflected in the Batavian Kong Koan Records." *Chinese Southern Diaspora Studies* 1 (2007).

Wall, Dr. V.I van de. *Oude Hollandsche Buitenplaatsen van Batavia.* Vol. Deel 1. Deventer: W. van Hoeve, n.d.

Wall, Dr. V.I. van der. *Oude Hollandsche Bouwkunst in Indonesie: Bijdrage tot de Kennis van de Hollandsche Koloniale Bouwkunst in de XVII-de en XVIII-de Eeuw.* Utrecht and Antwerpen: De Sikkel, Antwerpen and W. de Haan, Utrecht, 1917.

Wang, Ta-Hai and Walter Henry Medhurst. *The Chinaman abroad, an account of the Malayan Archipelago, particularly of Java.* London: J. Snow, 1850.

Ward, Kerry. *Networks of Empire: Forced migration in the Dutch East India Company.* Cambridge: Cambridge University Press, 2009.

Widodo, Johannes. *JAKARTA: a Resilient Asian Cosmopolitan City.* Singapore: National University of Singapore, n.d.

Wielenga, Friso. *Geschiedenis van Nederland: Van de Opstand to heden.* Amsterdam: Boom, 2017.

www.vocsite.nl, de VOC site. *Gegevens VOC-schip Walcheren 1612.* 5 February 2019.

Yamamoto, Mayumi. "Spell of the Rebel, Monumental Apprehensions: Japanese Discources on Pieter Erberveld." *Indonesia* October 2003, 76 ed.: 109–143.

Zahorka, Herwig. *The Sunda Kingdoms of West Java: From Tarumanagara to Pakuan Pajajaran with the Royal Centre of Bogor.* Jakarta: Yayasan Cipta Loka Caraka, 2007.

Zamzami, Irfan and Nila Ardhianie. "An end to the struggle? Jakarta residents reclaim their water system." Kishimoto, Satoko, Emanuele Lobina and Olivier Petitjean. *Our public water future: The global experience with remunicipalisation.* Vol. 40. Amsterdam, London, Paris, Cape Town and Brussels, 2015.

Zuidervaart, Huib J. and Van Gent, Rob H. "A Bare Outpost of Learned European Culture on the Edge of the Jungles of Java." *Isis* 95, no. 1 (2004): 1–33.

Acknowledgements

"I think you like your book more than you do me". That's what my wife Teni said one Saturday afternoon. That's obviously not true, but I realised it was time to put the book aside, shut the computer down and invite her and my son, David, out for a few drinks and a nice dinner. And that's what we did that evening. But for all the other weekends and late evenings that I spent digesting books and papers or just sat fixated staring at old maps, I thank her and David for being so patient with me. This book is dedicated to them.

The idea of writing a book had long been fermenting in my head. It all really kicked off after a Wednesday morning coffee with my colleague and friend, Jon Marsh. He knew of my idea to write a book on the history of Jakarta and he gave me some great tips. But the most valuable comment came as we threw the disposable cups in a bin and made our way back to our desks. At the elevator, Jon stopped and turned to me. "Writing", he said, "is the art of applying the arse to the seat." This was actually a quote from Dorothy Parker but also the best advice I got; if you want to write a book, you have to sit down and start typing. The following Sunday morning, I did just that. Jon had gotten me started. Much later, he gave me invaluable feedback after reading some of my early drafts. I am very grateful to him.

I also have to thank my father in the Netherlands, who tirelessly helped me to source books and maps. So did my uncle, Dinand, in Amsterdam.

He is the one who advised me in the 1990s to *not* start my backpacking trip in Jakarta (see the first chapter). He joined me on numerous visits to museums, libraries and small and sometimes obscure bookstores in Amsterdam, Leiden, The Hague and Hoorn. He also gave feedback and edits on my early drafts while cooking fantastic seafood paella and making his own tasty ginger beer. *Bedankt*!

In Jakarta, I am indebted to quite a few people. My nephew, Vandi, was willing to wake up well before dawn – before the heat and traffic descended each morning – to navigate me to a variety of arcane spots in the city where I wanted to identify an old grave, visit an ancient mosque or unearth remnants of a decrepit building. I also have to thank Diki for the generous use of his car and my sisters-in-law, Mbak Indah and Dini, who applied their fantastic social networking skills to arrange interviews with Jakartans who had a story to tell. The same goes for my aunt, Joes, and our friend, Mbak Ina. A few of those interviews took place in my brother-in-law Ucu's house, who also helped by generously making his unlimited supply of *kretek* cigarettes available to us. And I have to thank Ucu for getting soaked in heavy rain when, near midnight, I got stuck in a car in a small alley with a punctured tire and desperately needed help.

Dini also put me in touch with an organisation that promotes the local Betawi culture (the Lembaga Kebudayaan Betawi). There, I met Pak Beky Mardana and his friends – Pak Imbong Hasbullah, Pak Yahya Andisaputra and Pak Yoyo Muchtar – who provided me with lots of information with great enthusiasm. To all, I say "*Terima kasih banyak.*"

Others that helped me along the way are long-term Jakarta residents, James Brewis and Roland Haas, who connected me to Scott Merrillees, another author, and Che Wei Ling, the current owner of the Pancoran Tea House and a Jakarta history enthusiast. Pak Budi and Pak Harun at Museum Bank Mandiri showed me around their graceful buildings and gave me all kinds of historical information.

And then there are the numerous Jakartans who often unknowingly provided support or assistance, such as the residents of Rawa Bambu in Pasar Minggu, where I spent my early days in Jakarta. I am especially grateful to Fatma (she is the 9-year-old girl who got sick on a ferry in the first chapter) and her brother, Miman, who showed me around the alleys and local markets, and their incredibly hospitable parents, Mas Yadi and Bu Ati. The same can be said for many of the residents of Mabad II in Lenteng Agung.

Lastly, Anita Teo, She-reen Wong and the team at Marshall Cavendish International (Asia) have been extremely efficient and helpful with all kinds of technical matters involved in getting a book published and into bookstores. They also put me in touch with Brendan Whyte, who drew all the maps, and Derek Bacon, an illustrator whose beautiful pen drawing adorns the cover of this book. Thank you all.

Herald van der Linde

Index

A

B

O

observatory 103, 107, 144
Oger xviii, 120, 121, 125, 126
Ommelanden xx, 52, 54, 55, 60, 61, 63, 64, 65, 66, 67, 68, 69, 70, 71, 74, 75, 81,
    82, 84, 85, 88, 90, 91, 92, 93, 95, 98, 104, 107, 110, 132, 189, 205, 214, 216
ondel-ondel xviii, 119, 120
Ong Tae Hae 123, 124, 125, 126, 136, 190
Orang Betawi 68, 119, 120, 143, 163, 193
Order Baru 179
orphanage xiii, 46, 112, 122, 126

P

P.A. Daum 135
Pajajaran empire 12, 13
Pakuan xx, 13, 14, 15, 18, 19, 91, 218
Pancoran xiv, 32, 64, 65, 73, 74, 108, 116, 121, 173, 202, 216, 220
Pangeran Hadji 61
Pasar Baru xv, xviii, 119, 150, 151, 153, 185, 217
pepper 13, 15, 18, 19
Peranakan 38, 190
Petojo xv, 67, 114, 151, 163
Pieter Cortenhoef 43
Pieter Erberveld xvii, xx, 76, 77, 78, 79, 87, 101, 132, 163, 218
plantations 34, 35, 44, 45, 51, 58, 60, 61, 64, 67, 69, 72, 74, 82, 91, 105, 169, 189
Pluit 54, 57, 174
Portuguese xiv, 16, 18, 19, 20, 25, 40, 46, 47, 53, 62, 63, 71, 73, 74, 75, 77, 102,
    125, 154, 188, 213, 215
Pramoedja Ananta Toer 138, 196
Prasasti Tugu 11, 188
Preanger Bode 158
Prinsenstraat 31, 37, 38, 73
Purnawarman 10, 11

Q

Queen of the East 72, 82, 88, 126, 209

R

Raden Karta Dria 77, 79
Raden Saleh xviii, xxi, 128, 133, 134, 145, 151
Radio Dalam 167, 180, 186

Radio Republik Indonesia 175, 177, 178, 184
ramparts 30, 41
Reinier de Klerk xviii, 7, 97, 98, 102, 213
Rembrandt 202, 210
rijsttafel 126, 135, 153
Rijswijk 61, 62, 64, 66, 74, 82, 105, 114, 119, 121, 126, 131, 134, 135, 151, 175
rivers 9, 10, 14, 57, 68, 82, 84, 187, 189, 191, 194
River Sunter 65

S

Salak 9, 10, 13, 14, 72, 187
Sara Specx 43, 50
Sarwono 166, 169, 170, 172, 178, 185, 186, 206, 213
Sawah Besar 67, 83
Senen xix, 40, 66, 75, 83, 104, 105, 113, 118, 139, 150, 178
Singapore iv, xii, 1, 115, 132, 209, 210, 212, 213, 215, 218
Si Pitung xiii, xxi, 8, 139, 140, 141, 142, 143, 170, 206, 217
sirih 34, 35, 36, 60, 72, 94, 137
slaves xiii, 18, 19, 34, 58, 59, 60, 62, 63, 65, 69, 71, 72, 73, 77, 93, 97, 99, 105,
        106, 128, 193, 204
Souw Beng Kong vii, 25, 38
spin huis 46
Stamford Raffles xii, 115, 117, 121, 126, 132, 144
statues 103, 163, 172, 173
Stavinorus 91
sugar mills 60, 62, 63, 71, 82, 84, 85, 189
Suharto xxi, 152, 177, 179, 183, 184, 185, 209
Sukarno xxi, 161, 162, 163, 164, 165, 166, 168, 172, 173, 174, 176, 177, 178, 179
Sultan Ageng Tirtayasa 61
Sumatra 3, 10, 19, 130, 158, 162, 167, 206, 209
Sunda 7, 12, 13, 15, 22, 218
Sunda Strait 22
Sutan Sjahrir 162, 168

T

Taman Ismail Marzuki 134
Taman Prasasti 7, 79, 132
Tanah Abang 2, 41, 75, 83, 85, 86, 91, 118, 131, 132, 135, 139, 140, 141, 142,
        143, 151, 161, 181, 216
Tandjong estate 128
Tanjung Priok 134, 140, 148, 159, 168, 184
Tasmania 46

About the Author

Herald van der Linde is HSBC's Chief Asian Equity Strategist, also known as "The Flying Dutchman" given his frequent travels around the region. He and his Indonesian wife are based in Hong Kong and Jakarta. Prior to his role as a strategist, he had worked for 20 years in Indonesia, South Africa and Taiwan as an analyst. Herald is trained as an economist and wrote his Master's thesis in Jakarta. He decided to stay in the city after graduation and made it his home. This allowed him to extensively explore the Indonesian archipelago, which further nurtured his interest in the country and its history. Herald is a Certified Financial Analyst (CFA), speaks seven languages, including Bahasa Indonesia. He is also an Associate of the Institute of Wine and Spirits and is a certified lecturer for the Wine & Spirit Education Trust.